Don't Go Over the Bridge

Jaclyn Cohen

Don't Go Over the Bridge

Nanny Goat Hill

PRESS

FIRST EDITION
ISBN 978-0-5782-7919-0
ISBN(e-book)978-1-7923-9691-5

Designed and produced in the United States of America by New Standards Publishing Group

10 9 8 7 6 5 4 3 2 1

For Mariella:
B is for bridges. Build them. Burn them. Cross them.
And when in doubt, wear sunscreen.

Contents

Acknowledgments   ix

ONE   Don't Go Over the Bridge   1

TWO   On a Silver Platter   17

THREE   The Women's Club   41

FOUR   Yellow Tape   64

FIVE   Twitterpatted   95

SIX   Wall Art   126

SEVEN   Be Their Guest   149

EIGHT   The Caffeinated End   176

NINE   Fairy Wings   189

About the Author   201

Acknowledgments

It takes a village. And it's much easier when the village is your entire family, because they all live on the same block. No one's getting away with anything. And I thank them in no particular order, because if I ranked them, I'd be in big trouble:

My mother for her superb detective skills. The FBI should be so lucky. Hey, it's not easy raising daughters. Especially an inquisitive little bookworm with a whole lot of questions. And let's not forget my extra set of school uniform. "Never let them knock you down."

My daddy, for overtime, for car rides with extra cushioning, for my sweet tooth and funny bone. For our shared love of Hostess cupcakes, Ralph's Ices, pony rides, and rating Christmas decorations on the three-and four-honk system. "I'm taking the lawn chair."

My aunt—my godmother, my first hair stylist, my first boss, and savior of the backyard wildlife. For road trips with extra beach umbrellas, lobster bisque soup, pumpkin carvings, hot chocolate with whipped cream and sprinkles and a peppermint straw, teatime with Royal Albert, and just ALL the desserts. "Extra spray goes a long way."

My baby sister—my roommate for eighteen years and the reason for the invention of Squirrel Day. For wanting to come to my sixteenth birthday party, for borrowing my skirt, and for your interest in my sticker books. You just had to find my unicorns! Oh well, you know you're the cool one. "Stay sparkly."

My husband, my best friend, my love. You knew my addiction to Jane Austen and all things Mr. Darcy and still managed to marry me! For supporting me through the rough patches (kissing the booboos) and my dreams. Couldn't have done it without you.

My daughter, my heart, for bringing joy and meaning back into my life. Keep writing your stories. Make mistakes. Travel, travel, travel. Most important, always be you.

My in-laws, my family without the need of DNA, for keeping the fridge, pantry, and our hearts stocked. For the free babysitting hours that allowed me to create and polish this collection. Thank you for helping take good care of our most precious jewel.

My grandmother, my Mama Jack, the matriarch, the rock, the armor. For your open door, your open heart, your kitchen that never closed, for your volunteering and your dedication to the betterment of community, and a pair of listening ears that stretched for miles upon miles. It is a privilege and a blessing to have been loved by you. "It's either yes or no, never maybe."

My grandpa, my weatherman, my five-thirty in the a.m. wake-up call. For picking me up at school when I was sick, for checking the oil in my Chevy, and for lending some extra muscle when I needed it the most. Love your Bob Ross paintings, the way you tended to sick birds, and the bluest pool in all of Staten Island. "By the light of the silvery moon . . ."

My great-grandma, my grandmama, Lou, Lucy (and the many names you went by), the gift giver, for your kindness, goodness of spirit. For the best potato croquettes ever. Desserts, especially chocolate pudding graham cracker cake. "Go ahead, add a little salt. Say good morning and good night. Write the thank-you note. Call your mother."

All of my aunts, uncles, cousins, neighborhood friends, school friends, there are so many memories and thank-yous, I can't fit them all. (Don't yell at me.)

And last but not least, my furry editors, both canine and feline, but especially my tabby cat. (He is leaning over my shoulder as I type this.) For keeping me company on lonely afternoons and late nights while I drop cookie crumbs all over my keyboard.

Final thoughts:

Some families came by boat. Some by plane, ferry, car. Some drove over the bridge. No matter how they found their footing, they kept on moving forward.

———

Perry Avenue, thanks for the memories. This is a love letter to you.

···········

P.S. To that one nun, she knows who she is: Chicken Little made it!

Don't Go Over the Bridge

Don't Go Over the Bridge

PART I: BOYS AND A BRIDGE

"Don't go over the bridge," my mother tells me.

"You are not to go over that bridge."

My mother is a human lie detector.

"Do you understand?"

Capisce.

"Got it." I salute her.

No, Brooklyn. Bad, Brooklyn.

You have to understand. That bridge, that large suspension bridge is connected to that place.

It's connected to that land of far, far away. It's *the* land where my mother went to parties once upon a time. In the days of shimmery balls that hung from ceilings and pants that left little to the imagination. In the days of apartments filled with smoke and patrons who enjoyed lines of white powder, the non-confection kind.

She told me about this land and how she left the party early. How she finally had her fill of friends with sloppy noses and men who chased skirts. And what did she do?

Back over the bridge, back home she came.

She likes to remind me of the wickedness that lies beyond that bridge. Like this evening, parked in front of my best friend's house. I am sleeping over tonight, with a few friends from school.

I'd prefer to say that we're our own little group and not a clique, because we're not non-exclusive, it's more of a social setting put in place by the existence of the exclusives. We're awarded the designation of what I refer to as the "in the middle" crew: not exclusive enough to be on the tips of tongues of the entire student body— mind that we're only about eight hundred—but just enough to be invited to a few parties, and an occasional acknowledgment from the upper tier that we're not so unworthy of our own section of a rectangular table in the cafeteria. Not that it's such a rise above the other tables, because they all sort of blend into one specific theme: XX. As in the chromosome. This is not a surprise, because I attend high school with only girls.

That's correct. Only girls.

Most of the time it's totally cool, because there's always someone with an aspirin or a spare pad—forget the other kind, I don't like searching for strings—if I forget to pack my once-a-month fun supplies. I keep my hair in a bun four out of five days of the week. Okay, maybe five. I put on my glasses and I don't have to worry about wearing makeup. Or having to fix myself in the mirror—

And I'll never do that again. Sister Mary So-and-So caught me one time when I snuck a peek in my blush compact, and she sang aloud her rendition of Maria in *West Side Story*:

"SEE THE PRETTY GIRL IN THAT MIRROR THERE?"

Of course, there are also *girls*. And only *girls*. Girls with long fingernails, who scratch you as they grab the basketball from you and say: "But what are you doing?" Girls who yell at you to "Hit the goddamn volleyball over the net already!" Girls who fling mean words at weaker girls. Girls who ask what grade you earned on your test. Girls who drive expensive cars. Girls who never look your way or acknowledge your existence.

What's the missing ingredient?

Boys. Oh, boy. I sometimes forget they exist. But not if you were to see the inside of my locker. Boys from creeks, boys who meet the world, and a man who fought in the Colosseum.

But tonight, there will be boys. Real-life boys. Boys in the flesh.

My best friend has a boyfriend who lives in the forbidden land, and he is bringing friends. More boys from the forbidden land. They are coming across the forbidden bridge to meet us. When Henry Hudson took a longer route, he received a river. When Verrazzano anchored, he got a bridge. When the Lenape lived and fished there, fill in the blanks.

As I slam the car door, my mother waves. She waves with a pointed index finger. Pointing towards the forbidden. I nod again. *Do. Not. Cross.* The woman has the sixth sense. I'm convinced. Or maybe she's a secret agent.

The boys, they come out of the car. One of those older models with the full benches. Like those old-time movies where there's a boy who drives a large car (seriously, boat-size) and there's this rule or something that the girl's supposed to lean over and pull the lock up. Who made this up?

Not I.

But they are here. And they are already bored.

What are we going to do here? What's to do on this island? Our pizza is better. Our bakeries are better. Our bagels are better. The Mets. Everything is better over the bridge.

Some people on the island say that it was better here before the bridge went up. But that's not a nice thing to say. I didn't say it. I'm just reporting what I heard some people say.

"We're better off back there," said the group leader.

You always know the leader, because he drives the car. Simple fact. Just like the captain of the ship.

Back where? Back where, you say?

"The girls come back with us," the captain says to his crew.

"I can't go," I announce. If I say it out loud, I'll believe it, and therefore it must be true. My mind continues to ramble:

What if my mother calls the house? What if she finds out? What if I never see the light of day again?

Don't worry, they tell me. We'll only be gone awhile. Get something to eat, hang out. No worries. None. At. All.

Teenage girls give great advice. Teenage boys give even better advice.

Question: How do you fit nine teenagers in a car?

Answer: Why is there even a question?

Somehow, we ended up the way my elementary school teachers arranged us for special mass days: girl, boy, girl, boy, girl, boy. But instead of a pew, I sat on a lap.

Like Sister Mary So-and-So said one time, boys don't come with seat belts.

And this is how, I hear my mother say, *this is how you meet your end.* She didn't expect my end to be on the bridge. I didn't expect my end to be on a boy I didn't know.

He didn't mind. I could tell.

"Hey look, we can see our school," my best friend points, tapping the glass of the backdoor window. There she is, our fortress: a sturdy, stubborn, brownish brick building with Gothic-shaped windows. A gold cross balances on the gable of her chapel. Beneath the arch of her doorway, and above a stained-glass panel honoring the school colors, blue and gold, there is a saying engraved in concrete, it reads:

PARATE VIAM DOMINI

The chain-link fence bordering the property has three tiers of barbed wire. With the cost to secure the academy, I wonder its true purpose:

Stop the outsiders from getting in or keep the insiders from getting out?

The gymnasium and two red-brick buildings sit at the far end of the campus. Referred to by faculty and students as the annex, it's the oldest part of the academy and the hardest to reach when running late. And thanks to our proximity to the Verrazzano and the three standing-room-only lanes leading up to it that are somehow considered an expressway, I am super close to developing a chronic lateness for the rest of my senior year. Lucky me, I have an early class, as in forty-five minutes after seven in the a.m., in the annex, which has the worst kind of heating with white radiators that emit a snap and a crackle and a pop better than any cereal from a box and are counting down their final moments. Got to leave plenty of time for foot traffic, especially on snowy or icy days. I've seen more than one classmate end up flat on her rear, bare ass to the concrete, thanks to the minimal fabric that calls itself a skirt. Please don't mention stockings as a solution, because they're itchy and prone to runs with every tug, and there's always a need to tug, because its goal is either to suffocate my waist or slide down my crotch, and it's not like I can just pick it right back up without raising a few highly arched eyebrows.

And there was this time a girl from my honors class took an unforgettable spill, a Laurel and Hardy, slapstick-worthy kind of spill, while rushing to make gym class—not that I could blame her, because if you're late to the gym, you're going to be even later by the time it takes to remove all the parochial layers—pullover sweater, button-down oxford shirt, skirt with the zipper on the side, and the damn knee highs—to reach the required gray ensemble of cotton t-shirt and shorts. Then you have to balance with one hand on the locker to slip on your socks only to realize you left your socks at home and now have to wear the damn knee highs and look absolutely ridiculous right before the teacher, who, by the way, reminds you the importance of leaving your prior class promptly so as to give yourself the ample amount of time needed to trek in brown oxfords with no grip bottoms or arch support, and decides that the best punishment for you is to make up more time with dodgeball or kickball, or, shudder, volleyball, only for the jocks of the class to point out how much you suck at serving the ball. In my defense, my fine motor skills are better, more suited to flipping pages of paperbacks. Predominantly paperbacks involving nineteenth-century governesses escaping Byronic heroes across miles of a monotonous green wasteland.

Once, dormitories—the half-brick, half-cement buildings—housed an all-girl boarding school named after Saint John the Baptist. Where the boarders rested their heads is where I have art, Italian, and advanced placement English. It's an excellent setting for ghost stories. There's this one about a girl who could no longer live a life of restriction in small rooms guarded by black-and-white-attired faculty who were in possession of even smaller views. She found herself a one-way ticket and forever roams the halls of the school. And she pops in from time to time.

During a critical analysis (excuse me, analyses, since we all have an opinion, naturally) about a minister with an unusual fetish for a black veil—and if it wasn't for the veil, there would be nothing new to speak of among the parishioners in the Puritan village, aside from the local woman who's declared to be a witch—the blinds in our selective literature class were thrown open and slammed against the windows. We suspected our unrestful friend preferred Gilman over Hawthorne.

And who could blame her?

Oh, and then there's the infamous bathroom. Down the hall from art, on the first floor of the annex, there is a bathroom with grayish-green doors that, when closed, leave spaces too wide for comfort when I'm in the stall hovering over the bowl, regretting my liquid consumption. As I stand there, skirt above my waist, underwear at my ankles, I find that I am not alone. There is an image of a woman, her head veiled in white, who floats on a frosted window. She is known throughout the school as the Virgin Mary of the Annex. And her presence reminds the young maidens who pass her threshold of who we should be, yet fail to be, and eternal damnation if found out not to be—that is, until the blessed day when we walk down the aisle in white.

If I was to ever meet Our Mother, I do not want her first image of me to be a balancing act in a wide-gapped stall. I hope she doesn't see me now. I'm thinking that she wouldn't like this view of me, either.

The boy whose lap I am perched upon is wearing a headband. I want to ask him why he needs a headband on a seventy-degree evening. I don't. I prefer he'd not hate me the rest of the way.

The way over the bri—

We passed the point of no return: the green sign read "Exit 15 Lily Pond Avenue." No sight of the lily pads from here—only the upper level in view. I took a deep breath. If I hold my breath, it could keep me alive long enough if we went under. But I heard that if you hit the water, it's over. *Sayonara*, close the curtains, *finito*.

It's not like I haven't gone over it before. But never with a boy my age driving. And never on a boy's lap in the back seat. It's a whole other bridge tonight.

Soundtracks play in my head, a particular song of a cool guy who likes to walk in long strides and boogie down in dance halls. My mother and father are great dancers. They met in a disco. I did not inherit this gene. My sister can dance to Celtic music with flying toes and arms held straight against her body. I'm afraid she could topple and fall. She hasn't yet.

You know the legend of the bridge?

Some say there's a man who was buried alive in the foundation. Not true, Tony. But three men had fallen to their deaths during construction. Only after the last man's fall did the workers receive safety nets.

The view is clear tonight, and the lights of Manhattan are a welcoming banner. I mention that I haven't been there since last Christmas. To see *the* tree. Dependable, year after year, the tree is tall.

"Christ, you got to get off this island more," the boy in the passenger seat observes.

Try telling my mother.

"How about the promenade?" says the driver. "You've been there?"

I shake my head no.

"You haven't been to the promenade?" He raises his voice at the word of destination as if to suggest the ridiculousness of my situation.

"No, I haven't."

"How is that possible?" The captain and his first mate laugh.

Where is that crocodile when you need him? I can hear the tick tock, but it's probably my heart. Yes, it's my heart.

PART II: WHO'S THAT GIRL?

We found a spot.

"This is the Heights," says the boy whose lap has made my backside numb. When I finish stamping the pins and needles out of my legs, I take a look around.

The street is lined with brownstones. Not quite as brown as the name implies. Reddish, burnt orange, and tan. Each stoop starts at the sidewalk. Right on the street, no front lawns. No patch of grass to mow and complain that it's making me sneeze when my grandpa is out with the mower. Wrought-iron fencing with pointed spears guard the lower levels. I notice that the windows have bars. A few windowsills show their gentler side with flowers resting in boxes. There are potted ferns sitting on stairs and decorative railings leading up to the top step. The doors are enclosed in oval spaces with an overhang.

The knock on the door must be loud. I imagine standing beneath the chandelier—platinum setting, crystals shining over my head, like Belle in the ballroom scene when she swoops up her gold gown while the Beast holds his paw against the small of her back—and complimenting the hostess on such a fine fixture in her foyer when it hits me. Not the chandelier but that odd sensation that I've been someplace before. Déjà vu, is that you?

Wait a minute, I know this block. And I can see her. I can see her walking towards me. She has unbelievably high hair. Jet-black and curly. She's wearing red pumps and she just kicked a soda can. I have always wanted to wear red heels and kick a soda can. But I only have on black slides, so this is not going to work.

I explain this to my friends and the boys who have taken us to a land where Cher once walked.

Oh, to be Loretta in the red pumps. Red pumps worn to the opera. If you have to make an entrance, that's how it's done.

My seat mate regrets to inform me that this is *not* the block, that block is over a few. He mumbles something about me being such an islander. It turns out, the street where Cher strode in red pumps is a fruit of a different name.

The driver grabs my friend by the hand and they return to the car. I am left to wander around with the rest of the pack and pretend to know where I am. The boys take us to the water view. There's a line of benches, and the pavers are hexagon-shaped. Nighttime has arrived, and love is on parade.

There are couples holding hands, walking the promenade and discussing their life plans. One couple is sitting on a bench overlooking the East River. She leans her head against her lover's chest, his arm cradled around her. I wonder if I'll ever be able to do the same, to describe the way a chest rises and falls. Or know the weight of an arm around my shoulder and the way his fingers dangle as I entwine them with my own.

Manhattan is bright and close. I can reach out and draw an outline of her figure. I make sure to keep the corners tight as I climb each building. There are four long vertical lines as I come to the highest point in the center. I walk my fingers across each pair as if I'm a tightrope walker.

Like a nosy neighbor, I peer inside her windows. The people are under her spell: busy feet treading the sidewalks, weaving in and out of herds, stopping only at corners for an orange hand, and continuing onwards, uptown or downtown, on a series of gridded blocks and underground tunnels, and during that time being cautious not to make eye contact and, overall, avoiding what little engagement is possible with the other beings in herds so that the members of the many herds can make it to their destination on time.

Each individual belongs to a greater herd, each man, woman, and child scurrying among the packs, participating in internal commentary: a list of the items they'd like for lunch, caffeine is number one; notes on the many ways fellow human beings spread contagion—*Did you see that man with his finger up his nose?*—members of the herd who dare to slow the pace of the group, like the bewildered tourist who stops to snap pictures and steps on someone's heel; moments of *Why is it only Monday?* (or Tuesday, Wednesday, or Thursday, for that matter); and most important on the internal list of criteria is the pre-planning of weekend festivities.

And what type of festivities will be predicated upon the said individual being either (a) an introvert, which would most likely land them in fuzzy pants with remote in hand or, better, a book and a furry creature for company, or (b) an extrovert, sitting on a stool in a bar or dancing on a floor caked in sticky overflow from drinks held in one hand and cigarette in the other by people of the greater herd whom they hope to engage but purposely dodge from Monday to Friday.

As for who I may be, either (a) or (b), I am imagining my coziest pair of pajamas and slippers. If I had a fairy godmother, I'd wish to be bibbity, bobbity, booed and given a pair of Brookstone slippers, the kind that mold to your foot. It's like walking on mattresses. And I would know if there was a pea.

PART III: PAY THE TOLL

It's midnight, but I'm still me. I made it back over the bridge, all limbs still attached. I counted.

I'm sitting at the curb where I was earlier with my mom and her pointed index finger. The boys have returned to their land of origin. I should be happy, thrilled that I beat the system. I conquered the bridge, I conquered my mother. Who does she think she is, telling me when or where I should or shouldn't go? I'm practically grown, practically an entire woman—minus the ultimate experience of womanhood, as a few of my peers who have already partaken divulged in great detail.

So, what is this feeling that sits on my chest? It is beginning to gnaw a little hole in my stomach as well. While one of my friends stamps out a cigarette, I take time to prepare my confession. Because that's what we do. We do the things we were told not to do and then we confess with preestablished words, followed by more words spoken in a particular order for a certain number of times, and that is the answer of how I will sponge the deed away.

A DAMSEL
sometimes I wonder
if I wore
my sins like armor
I'd be a knight
instead of a damsel
stuck in my tower
waiting for magic
to escape

SECRET KEEPER

when I sit upon my chair
I find
a man behind a screen,
a secret keeper, I am told
to whisper in his ear
the truest truths spoken
no exits to fear
but what will happen
to those rotten eggs
that pile by the day
no curtains can contain
the secret keeper,
what will he do
with the walking talking shame
the forsaken
the taking of the Lord's name
shove them into his pockets
cram them in good—

does he own pockets?

maybe he's got a net
for catching butterflies
scoop each one by surprise
the light ones float
away like dandelion wisps
at the breeze
but what about the secrets
the ones that drop like
anvils and shake the ground
when they hit
they crack the foundation

but secret keeper,
poor secret keeper
sometimes I've been told
he's been made to disguise
grizzly hides
big enough to swallow up
the earth
in one large gulp
like a giant toad
on a giant lily pad
and I imagine that he
the man, the cloth,
the man and his cloth
venture into the toolshed

does the rectory have a toolshed?

and finds a shovel
digs a hole
six, eight,
ten feet deep
and pats the grizzly hides
down good
real good
not a hair out of place
but sometimes
I fear
it doesn't stay down
it won't lie down
and die
like it should
the way the good sins do
and then the secret keeper

needs to get resourceful
super resourceful
and go into a drawer
maybe a dresser drawer
maybe a communal junk drawer
like in the kitchen—
I suppose he gets together with all
the other secret keepers
and they have coffee
with cream
sometimes half and half—
and he shuffles around until he finds
a book of matches
he's trying to quit
but nicotine is hard
harder than the secrets to keep
and sometimes they chase after each other
the secret keeper
goes outside with the big pile
of rotten eggs, grizzly hides,
some butterfly wings mingle in
and he secures them all to a stake
and lights the match
sits and watches
the smoke rise
he'll wait around—
probably until dusk
or until dinner because
all this secret business has
got him feeling famished—
until the ashes fall and
he can sweep them into a
glass jar

a pretty mason jar that
he'll store with the rest
in the cellar
to be decorated by the
common brown house spider
until somebody decides to
go and be a busybody and dust
the cellar shelves and accidently
break open a glass jar and
allow the monsters to run free
it's a shame really
they made a big mess
and nearly ruined the carpets
in the rectory

but secret keeper,
if only you knew the rules
of laundering
how there's nothing worse than a stain on
white
even my mom tried so hard
to wash the cola
I spilled
on my communion gown
but there's nothing
I mean nothing
to take it out
lemon
seltzer
bleach
you can try
but it's always going to be there

TWO

On a Silver Platter

ON A SILVER PLATTER
there was a head
on a silver platter

I turned the page fast
but then I turned back
each time it was worse
his eyes
closed
his hair
curly
his beard
thick
the cut
fresh
splotches of red
dripped onto the silver platter
held by an amorous woman
wrapped in a white gown

――――

she presents the leader
with the prize
the tetrarch is pleased
he is happier
each time I return to the page
and I must remember
to skip over this story
I can rewrite history
with my false eye
when I move my laminated bookmark
with the purple tassel

there's a savior
on the front cover
dressed in a long white robe
a yellow glow surrounds his head
his eyes
blue
his hands
raised
fingers to the sky

inside the hardcover edition
stories unfold from old
to new

once upon a time
a king
holds up a baby
with his muscular arm
the woman at his left side
reaches for the swaddle
the woman on his right side

is on her knees
as he draws his sword close
to the infant

in a kingdom faraway
a man
with long hair
stands next to a lion
he is chained to a column
the lion wears
an open-mouth smile

tales
I was gifted
as a little Christian
the first time I knelt
I practiced the Act
of Contrition
I recited the lines to a man
in a purple and green robe
and given homework

my hands
folded
over the pew
my knees
rested
on a cushion
I was awarded a pin
mother squeezed its wings
to fit my collar
a small hole
laid in cotton
polyester blend

the pin
held a figure of a man
with nails
through his wrists and feet
on two beams of wood
the same display
in the center of the church
the one baptized
by he
who lost his head
to the silver platter

SKY WRITER
paint brush

containers of red
orange
yellow
blue
green
indigo
violet

a canvas

how angels are taught
to paint the sky

THE DISCOUNTED
dear mistress
of the popsicle sticks,

on my honor
I will try
not to drip
as I dip
into the milky white paste
squeezed
from the bottle with an orange cap
to twist
the dairy cow laughs
when I stir like
there's a secret recipe
inside the Styrofoam bowl
and I will not cackle
and pretend that it's a cauldron
not ever, I swear—
even though
it's October
and I'm dreaming
in peanut butter cups—
I know if I listen and
act like the good scouts
around me
I may reach great
ecclesiastical heights

the girl beside me—
who is too popular to give me an extra
chocolate munchkin
even though it is her birthday and she could
try to be nice—
rolls her eyes
turns up her nostrils
and moves her elbow from mine

———

you're weird,
she mumbles as she reaches
for the non-glue side
of the stick that goes in your mouth
at the doctor's
when he takes it from the glass jar
next to the cotton balls
the leftovers come here
hoping to graduate with a green beret
and parade around in a tan sash

how many badges do you have?

at least I made it to the brownies
although I don't like nuts
this troop is definitely walnuts
and no matter how many times I wish
they'll never taste like the Milky Way

and now here comes part two:
when you're finished with the glue
I'm not finished on time
I never am
too many people in here
doing too many people things
and how can I want to glue
when I'd rather look at what the others do:

and did you hear that John likes Jane?
she's pretty
you're not
she has a shape
and yours forgot your name
can you blame him?

you can't see a thing
put your purple rim frames back on,
purple girl
weird purple girl with the matching
purple jacket that grows past your knees
you look
like that big dinosaur
your little sister watches on that station
the one that's funded by the nation
oh, mother
thanks for the coat

and where is that woman?
I'm not allowed to walk down the block
alone
since little Jennifer was found in Willowbrook
snatched in the broad daylight
dad says you can never trust
anyone on the street
don't say hello
don't look them in the eye
an urban
lullaby

well, she's taking the glue away
I guess I'm finished—
here's a bowl of green paint

dear mistress
of tan sashes,
have you heard that Styrofoam
hurts the earth
and the garbage dump can be seen from space?

no?

———

I got my paintbrush, thanks

dear mistress
of the paint supplies,
on my honor
I will take this green paint
and smear it across my face
where I'll wear it proudly
when I run across the playground
they lock us in
for about forty-five
minutes in designated spots
reserved on Sundays
it's a parking lot

and if you're unlucky enough
to be caught by
the warden of the concrete land
for doing something
out of hand
she's a firm one alright
gray hair with
a chin that sprouts
she'll make you pay upright
she shouts:
stand tall and still
like a tree, a miniature
obedient tree, planted on a
yellow line drawn
for full-bench Oldsmobiles and a Marquis,
the blue Mercury kind
I sit in the middle and watch my poppy
fiddle the shift to drive

and you had better not step off that line
warden watches you from behind
otherwise, it's hands and knees for you
up until three on a Saturday afternoon
ten Hail Marys
and an Our Father, please

where's my mother?
doesn't she know it's almost time?
I count it by the minute
5, 4, 3, 2, and 1
little shamrock left
in the chapel
beneath the stairs
that lead to the garden
where three children
and their flock of sheep
surround a woman
in a cloak
to whom they pray,
the one they call
the Virgin

I see her,
my mother
but she doesn't look as if
she agrees with my new shade
of evergreen scout
I believe it will grow on her

I hope it has

THE BAND-AID
there's a turtle with a Band-Aid
in the backyard,
I tell my godmother

the turtle has a pink Band-Aid
for a bridge
its shell split down the middle
with orange and black splotches
to play reptilian hopscotch

a Band-Aid?

yes, a Band-Aid

godmother
who is also my aunt,
mom's big sister,
when they used to play
grandma said
my aunt liked to run
mom fell behind
no arches to her soles
flat feet, I suppose
I'm a turtle offspring too

godmother and I
gather at a patch of green earth
grown mobile
his belly skims the lawn
and I wonder if he is aware
of the fluorescent mark
on his mode of transportation
the only shell he'll call home

———

he must have escaped from another yard

maybe he was run over

or dropped?

we discussed the possibilities
he may have followed
the turtle trail

my aunt and uncle have a turtle trail
in their backyard
the turtles are a seafoam green
sometimes I hop along the turtles
leap from one stone to the next
so my toes are never tickled by the grass
and wander
under an archway of vines
where the fairies climb
to nestle in lilac beds
and soon he'll fall
deep in love
swayed by the scent of a vegetable garden
with grape tomatoes and
basil for sauce
the aroma of the leaves
stay on my fingertips
oh and carrots,
Victory-style
like the ones they used to grow
back in the days of World War II
I read that in a textbook
the textbook still has the USSR
stamped across the world map

and there's a list of names
of the students before me
who read it and signed their names into history
my name's in there too
for an eternity,
like forever and a day,
or until they're trashed
for a new edition

but the turtle trail
never moved until today
the turtle was real

what should we do?

we can't leave him behind
roaming the neighborhood
in a Band-Aid
he'll be a laughingstock of all the fauna
and the flora
should we let him be bullied?
the blue jays squawk
the squirrels twitch their tails
and my entire pet cemetery of betta and goldfish
beneath the evergreen and oak tree
roll over in their little soiled graves
and they'll never be the same
we
cannot
have
that

godmother makes a bed
out of a box
adds some grass for his scaly head

I like him
he's cute
even with the pink Band-Aid
and a crater for a shell

I'll hold him in the car, I say, hugging the box that once
stored a pair of shoes

if turtles had to wear shoes
would they need a pair for their front legs
and back legs?
that could get expensive
I think it's better
that he doesn't need them
although if he had sneakers
he could have outrun whatever it was
that made someone think
hey, let's slap on a Band-Aid
that'll work

we'll take him to Northside—
they help exotics, my aunt says, leaning over to adjust
the car seat strap cradling her firstborn

exotics?

I wonder . . .
if he's lucky
there'll be palm trees inside
to fan him and
he could use a little relaxation
I can see him
sitting in a lounge chair
drink at his side
sipping from a swirly straw

the roller-coaster type that's fun
to watch your soda twist in loops
when I put in a fancy mini umbrella
he smiles

my little cousin
points to the turtle
and me,
we're in the back of the
Grand Marquis
my uncle drives us to a red house
on Post Avenue
once in art class
I saw a painting of
a man near a red house
his eyes were wide open
white and round
eyebrows and moustache
were brown
red pupils
and a frown
I don't know why
but he was only a head

let's have a look here,
says the man in a white lab coat

he lifts the patient from the shoebox
the turtle drops his straw
lab coat man scratches his chin
when he sees the fluorescent attire
maybe he prefers a different color
pink is too bright against orange and black
yellow is a better choice

_____

this sir, he says, cradling the bandaged patient,
needs a little extra care
we'll transport him to our friends
at William T. Davis

I'm relieved to learn
he'll make friends at the refuge
he needs comrades
those who understand
his coldblooded need to retreat
when life grows
too worrisome
too fast
not a thought lost to the taunts of
those who scorn
those who scoff his slower pace:
haven't they read who won the race?

once he is back in shape,
he'll be returned to the wild,
the doctor examines the patient's flippers

I knew he should have worn shoes
I picture the turtle performing
calisthenics
like we do in gym class
as my teacher eats donuts for motivation
but without the jumping jacks
I don't think he could jump rope either
maybe he'd be good at push-ups
I bet he's excellent at those

you're safe here,
I whisper,

but I have tears in my eyes
I'm a fool
to fall so fast
I've succumbed
to reptilian charms
grown accustomed to his wayward shell
but I remember that he was never
and could never
be mine

you won't be alone for long,
I say,
a pair of latex hands
take command and I am left
only to juggle thoughts
of pink and green
sneakers and straws

I can tell you are already
the star
the teacher's pet
the long-lost son who has suddenly
reappeared
but what's not to like
about a turtle adventurer
who enjoys the tropics and
is great at push-ups?

**BETWEEN THE BIG TOE AND
THE SECOND TOE**
don't ever paint your toenails
with your cousin on a summer evening

it doesn't matter what color you paint your toenails,
don't ever leave your grandparents' house without flipflops

you can risk the smudge on your big toe

don't climb down the wooden staircase
between the Japanese maple trees
after you painted your toenails with your cousin
on a summer evening

you can giggle all you want—
put on your flipflops first

don't run across the red brick pathway
lined with azalea bushes
after you climbed down the wooden staircase
between the Japanese maple trees
that border the property of
your grandparents' ranch with the purple shutters and
your aunt's house with the tall magnolia tree
that drops pink and white petals along a lattice fence
on the summer evening
you painted your toenails with your cousin

you own flip flops in five different colors
pick a pair, please

don't be shocked when
you feel a slimy squish between your big toe
and your second toe—
which happens to be smaller than your big toe,
not a common trait in your family where the second toe,
the Grecian toe, is longer than the first

neither toe minds the thong
of a flip flop

———

don't scream when you witness the horror
that awaits when you reach the side entrance
of your aunt's house to discover
the identity of the slimy squish between your big toe
and non-Grecian second toe

MIGHT YOU RECONSIDER THE NECESSITY OF
    A PAIR OF SUITABLE
FOOTWEAR?

don't cry when you look down
to find that you are a giant:
fee
fi
fo
fum
to a brown and black spotted invertebrate
leisurely making his way home
a trail of glistening perspiration that lay in his wake
now belongs to the bottom of your foot

don't lift your unattired foot and
beg your aunt for immediate assistance
pleading:
GET IT OUT!
GET IT OUT!
and realize
you should have risked the smudge on your big toe

still prefer a smudge to a squish, do you?

don't complain that you won't ever go barefoot again
at the funeral of the
brown and black spotted invertebrate

you mercilessly squished between your big toe
and non-Grecian second toe
on the red brick pathway lined with azalea bushes
pink and white magnolia petals strewn to commemorate
the misfortune
all because you painted your toenails with your cousin

don't ever
trade your flip flops
for nail polish
and don't ever
trust your soles to a summer's night

POTS AND PANS
the pots and pans
they can be heard
at midnight
when the ball drops in Times Square
a spoon meets the backside of
grandma's saucepan
and a ladle sings
inside the pot where
she reheats the lentils
two days old
from the freezer
open the side door
and bang for all to hear:
happy new year!
we scream
happy new year!
with love from my family
happy new year!

with love from my large Italian-American family
who made the journey generations before
their hearts clanging in their chests
in an unfamiliar land
of unfamiliar people

and tonight it's all of us
saucepans, pots, and ladles
we hear a clanging from across the expressway
there's a man flicking his porch light on and off
he screams:
happy new year!

we clang in return
flick our porch light
on
off
on
off
lights, pans, pots, and cheer . . .

Neighbors

"I'm not saying hello." Lana folds her arms across her chest. I notice that her shirt has the same logo as my own. Hilfiger. With capri pants that fall right below the knee and a pair of black platform sandals, we may as well be twins. I guess that thing sort of happens when you shop at the same department stores.

"Why not?" I don't understand why she's making a fuss.

"Because it's weird."

"It's not *that* weird."

"But it *is*," she insists.

I met Lana freshman year. Since we both have last names that begin at the start of the alphabet, we sit at the Homeroom 1 table in the cafeteria.

"I only want to say hi and then leave. I promise." I hold up three fingers, crossing my thumb over my pinky. "Scouts honor."

Lana sighs. She crosses the street without checking if any cars are coming. I check three times before my foot is off the curb. Right, left, right.

"Wait up," I call out.

We clicked, friends at first sight. You know when you know—

she wore a scrunchie on her wrist too. Lana had curly hair like me. And she didn't seem to mind me sitting near her even though I wore my purple frame glasses and a set of barrettes. They were floral and sparkly and placed me in the category of prudes. (That's code for never been kissed. The tongue kind.) It only took forever to grow out a bad haircut. Those damn banana bangs. My mom is from the heated rollers generation, so she enjoys hairspray and high (really high) hair.

"Where are they?" Lana raises her hands in question.

"Go down one."

It's not that my family is estranged or that there's any bad blood. I never met them. Not formally, anyway. (Unless photos count.) But with everyone's busy schedules and, well, life, I wasn't gifted the opportunity. And with the discovery of Lana living in such close proximity—try across the street—it is my familial obligation to introduce myself. My only regret is not coming prepared. Number one rule in Italian families: always bring a gift when you visit. Empty-handed visitors are frowned upon. But this was a surprise. "I think I found them," I say, walking past a mound of freshly laid dirt.

"Let me see."

I kneel down and point to a pair of names. Lana wipes a brown smudge from her sneaker as she leans over me.

"This *is* weird," she says.

"No. It's family."

"Who are they exactly?"

"My great-grandparents. My poppy's parents."

"Oh. Can we go now?" Lana looks over her shoulder.

I glide my hand across the stone of my ancestors. I trace my mother's surname.

"Sicily."

"What about it?"

"That's where they're from." But they had no bridge, they came by boat.

"It's getting dark." Lana's shoulders quiver. She rubs them back and forth and stamps her feet. Fall has made an appearance.

"Pizza?"

"Yeah."

"Blockbuster?"

"Yeah."

Good-bye, great-grandma.

Good-bye, great-grandpa.

Don't say hello tonight.

THREE

The Women's Club

THE WOMEN'S CLUB
here's a $5,
grandma's younger sister hands me
a slip of green paper
buy yourself some powder puffs

I find it odd that I will use Lincoln
as a monetary exchange
for adhesive bandages
that sit between my thighs

welcome to the women's club,
great-aunt kisses me good-bye
wow,
is it like a resort?
can I swim in blue water
and drink from coconuts?

I want to put a straw in a coconut
like in the cartoon

when the smart-talking bunny gets stranded
on a deserted island
and then I can wear the discarded
coconut shells
as a bathing suit top
but it won't hold up
no way
even if I drink more milk
it never did my body
any good
it would be cool to wear clamshells though
and run a fork through my hair
this is all possible now
because my pituitary gland said it is finally time
to release an egg
an amazing egg
better than any golden egg
laid by a goose
and everybody wanted that goose

will I be popular now too?

POODLE ON PARADE
PART I

pink foam rollers are the worst
forget sleep
there's no sleeping with rollers in my hair
that mom insists I wear
no matter the protest
how hard I resist
she weaves the pink foam
through each strand

try not to admit it—
I look a bit like Frenchy

but no other ladies in pink arrive
no sleepover tonight
I toss and turn
only my stomach will do
cause they tug
those rollers
they tug and they pull
even worse than when a strand
of hair gets caught in one of the
round silver screws that sit
in the back of my chair
in the wooden desk at school
the desks face forward
five straight rows
textbooks in storage
underneath my seat
neatly stacked by order:
smallest on top
largest at the bottom
a book tree wrapped
in brown paper bags
the paper bag may come in handy because
it's picture day—
that's why I have the rollers
the pink foam rollers make an appearance for
every holiday
they surround my entire head
and I may be able to get reception
change channels with my pink rollers
there'd never be a need for antennae

the bunny-ear kind
we still have a television with retractable ears
in the second bedroom
I watch it when the living room TV
is stuck on *60 Minutes*
or when I've had enough of Rather and Walters'
perfect vision

if aliens landed in my house
and demanded to abduct my family
they'd see my rollers and know
that I am already one of them
unmistakably not an Earthling
Earthlings are not known for twisted pink
appendages growing out of their head
so on a positive note,
I am saving my family
I will sacrifice my sleep
in case the night comes
when we are visited
and if that doesn't work
I will remove each roller by hand
and when I reach the last strand
my locks will transform and seek revenge
because now I am Medusa
and I will turn them all
to stone
what's that, mom?
oh, it's time to leave?
great, I can't wait to arrive.
look nice on picture day, self.
I have to hand out the 4-by-6 prints
to the entire family

pick out a background:
blue or green?
blue is nice
blue swirls bring out the poof
in my hair
and she wants to make it bigger:

how much bigger, mom?

aerosol spray is bad
for the ozone
and I already have a few layers
to spare with these
precious curls she adores

why do they look so big?

don't mind me
she keeps on spraying
I cover my eyes
and close my mouth
but too late—
I taste the sticky residue

don't touch them,
my mother instructs,
swatting my fingers away
from a curl that bounces
like a Slinky
upstaging my eyebrow

let them fall naturally,
she says, adding another spritz

but if you wanted them to
fall naturally,

why did I have to wear
these in the first place?

just get in the car.

got it.

PART II

I arrive at school—
if Hades had another level,
it would be seventh grade

nice hair,

says a boy who sits behind me
with dimples when he smiles
the dimples make him cuter
but I'm not going to tell him

he pats my hair like they do
at the Westminster Kennel Club
checking for regulation length

you look like a poodle.

thanks for pointing it out
to the class
and on further thought,
your dimples are not cute
not impressive in the least

just wait for the class photo, he says
I'll hide behind you
pretending to part the Red Sea with my hair
like Charlton Heston in *The Ten Commandments*

———

that's funny,
I pretend to laugh

laughing hurts better
than pink foam rollers

THE CALL
my aunt from Indiana called
asked dad about the weather
he said something about it being hot
I'm not sure what is so fascinating about the weather
but adults have the need
to discuss atmospheric conditions
at the start of every call

a storm named Bertha had
barreled through
she left a puddle on our street
for the pigeons to wade in
and an occasional seagull, but they prefer
sand and not concrete
I want galoshes
to make a splash
but galoshes aren't the statement to make
in the afternoon
in July
in New York City
it's just not cool

my dad holds the wire curled
around his hand
like a long fusilli strand

and stands
one foot crossed in front of the other
I wait my turn
to tell my father's eldest sister—
whose skin is fair and who has red hair
like Ann with an *e* who reads poems when she walks
around a lake with shimmering water—
that I finished the book she sent me in the mail
it was great
I didn't tell my mom and dad that the book
talked about boys and periods
and breasts not growing fast enough
and the girl she's sort of like me
with the questions
asking questions that don't have answers
like when I asked a cloud its opinion
or talked to a ripple in a chlorinated pool

but dad leaves the phone
alone
the receiver knocks
into the wall and all
because of the sirens
the sirens sing
and it shouldn't matter
they sing
around the clock
morning
noon
and night
even three, four, and
five o' clock
before dawn

they drift along
like the beat of a song

except today
the symphony is
so close it could be a newborn
wrapped in a swaddle
its cries echo
down the block
and shake my living room floor
I search
from the balcony
a crowd gathers on the sidewalk
behind the linked chain
that separates
our street from the flow
of cars on Bradley Avenue
a yellow sign sits in the center,
it reads:

DEAD END

from my second story
I investigate:
there's a man in khaki shorts
he shakes his head
next to an older gentleman whose
belly peeks out over
his belt
beside a woman,
her mouth is hanging open
like a fly trap
and the neighbors from up the block
a toddler grasping her

mother's leg
join the school of gawkers
pointing towards the traffic light
at the corner
while a parade
of cars stands still
the windows lower—
drivers poke out their
noses like eager little
groundhogs bent on spoiling
green turf

a man with a megaphone,
squeezes himself between
all those noses,
pointed fingers, and squinted eyes
a director to the crowd
of rubber necks:

let 'em through!
a cacophony of sirens
join the chorus

when my father returns
I have a million questions
I want to know
why the entire neighborhood
chose to leave their homes
and telephones
to stop and listen together
to the sirens' song
that's still ringing
in my ears

———

why can't I see?
I insist
it's not for young eyes.
young eyes?
thanks to a myopic disposition
I have glasses with a high prescription
they're thick enough,
I should be safe

I want to see.
no.
is it bad?
dad's lips remain closed
as I inch towards the blinds

there's a girl in the back of the car,
he whispers to my mother
my mom feeds my little sister
while she watches a dinosaur
sing and dance on television
the purple dinosaur wears a hat
and carries a magic stick

a young girl, he says
I part the pink verticals
that shield our second-story window
from the afternoon glare
one beam has carved a path to
the kitchen table

young? mom repeats,
cutting my sister's chicken cutlet
into toddler-size bites
and she's not alone.

they didn't see it coming?
no.
they didn't hear it?
their radio was loud.

they didn't hear what? I ask,
walking my fingers through the
sunbeam because
I like to catch the dust
the fire truck, mom says, piercing a piece
of chicken with a fork

the front page
of the newspaper reads:
taken too soon
a mother and daughter
call home

The Instructor

"But I can't skate," I tell my dad, gripping the side of the rink. My fingers are whiter than the block of ice that has claimed my mobility for its own amusement.

The rink is located inside a large white arena in the shape of a bubble. It makes me crave marshmallows in hot cocoa with a big swirl of whipped cream on top. I'll add some rainbow sprinkles.

"Let go and move your feet," Dad says, standing behind the tempered glass.

"I'll land on the ice again. On my butt." I point to my sore bottom. "That hurt and it probably left a bruise."

Ugh. Curse my weak ankles. The truth is that I don't mind trading a pair of skates for a spot on the bench. There's nothing wrong with preferring benches. My feet are safe. My legs aren't sore. And it's an excellent spot to pick up the chapter where I left off. I keep a book with me at all times for just-in-case moments. Or events requiring public participation, or anything classified as a sport. My copy of *The Saddle Club* is waiting in my bag and I never tire from reading about horses. But skates? These rentals wear me out.

"All that work to put them on and now you want to leave?"

"It wasn't my idea, and didn't you hear about the boy who fell on the rink?"

"Who?"

"The boy."

"What boy?"

"Some boy, Dad. He couldn't get himself up in time and another skater sawed off his finger."

"Who told you that?"

"Everyone knows that story."

"That's a tale."

"I need my finger."

I envision a red pool forming on the ice. The detached limb lies there like a discarded branch. I will not be the next red pool. I will not be the next tale to be told at a safety meeting. I cannot return a pair of white rentals in splotches of my own blood.

"How about *you* teach me to skate?" I point at my dad.

He walks along the side of the rink with the other warm-blooded creatures who still have full usage of their fingers and toes. Dad stands before the opening, inspecting the frozen pool of impending doom. He watches as the dozens of people who have joined me zoom their way around the rink. A bunch of light-footed penguins. But what does it matter now? We'll be leaving in a minute and I'll be one step closer to a cup of hot chocolatey goodness. Rejoice.

"Haven't worn skates since before you were born. I have to make it into work," Dad says, still scanning the ice for cracks. Or whatever it is that makes clumsy daughters fall on their backsides. Piece of advice: listen to your mom when she says to wear leggings under your pants.

"Can we leave?" I ask. I want to punish the ice and these stupid skates. As soon as I can let go of the rink. But my fingers aren't getting the message. And neither are my feet.

"Hold on a minute." He holds up his pointer finger. "I'll be right back."

"Don't leave me here. I'm—"

But he is already gone. All that is left to do is people-watch. Just stand—well, lean—and blend. Become a part of the wall. Blending should be a sport. Or devising a formula for invisibility, now that would be even better.

There's a five-year-old on skates and he's making me look bad. He races from one side of the rink and back, trying to get his sister's attention. His sister has given up on him to talk to a boy her own age.

My age.

They are cozy. She is wearing a fuzzy sweater and he's in a fleece hoodie. Oh, he made her laugh. She grabs his arm and he spins her. She laughs again. What's funny anyway? What could be so amusing about skating in a rink that's a little bigger than our kitchen sink?

"Hey, I have a surprise." Dad interrupts my view. Too bad I'll never know how their relationship ends.

"I hired an instructor."

Say that again.

"What did you do?"

"He's on his way."

"No, no. I want to go."

And in slow motion, like a dramatic entrance from one of those romantic movies that my grandma and my mom like to watch on Lifetime and Hallmark—he walks towards the rink. White jersey, black pants, and just—oh, do I want to run at this moment but I'm as frozen as a red, white, and blue firecracker popsicle—no mistaking, he's all boy.

No. He is an *older* boy, like one who is on the corner of being a man. I heard that expression once: *He's on the corner of boyhood and manhood.* Whatever corner he is on, I'm glad he stepped off the curb.

He glides onto the ice. There's definitely signs of stubble. Possibly a five-o'clock shadow. Not exactly sure what that looks like but he doesn't have a smooth baby face like the boys in my elementary school.

And he is tall, so tall that I have to lift my chin up and squint to see him. I left my glasses in my coat pocket because they are uncool. I'm glad, because this guy is so cool.

How old is he? He has to be in high school. Like the end of high school, after the SATs. I'm studying so I can be accepted into Catholic high school. I could tell him that.

Just don't drool. I didn't know guys could look like you.

And he's got a cute boy haircut. His hair is shaved underneath and the rest of his blond locks float on top. Kind of like a mushroom.

He grabs my hands. "Don't be afraid."

I watch as the wall moves farther away. I am miles away.

My dad waves. I know exactly what he's thinking and I'm hundred percent sure he has zero clue what I'm thinking. Otherwise, he would never dangle a boy in front of me like a carrot. He waves again. *Isn't she precious? I just want to pinch those cheeks.* That kind of wave. Is there a blanket I can hide under?

What are these? Calluses, thick calluses. And all ten fingers.

"Let yourself glide," the older boy says. "Move your ankles like mine."

He demonstrates moving left and then right.

I'm curious what it says on his shirt. Something with a puck.

"What do you do?" I ask.

"I play hockey here every week."

I might have a new appreciation for this sport.

"And you give lessons?"

"Not really," he smiles, as I lose sensation in my knees. "But your dad asked me."

Thanks, Dad.

"So, is that okay with you?"

Well, duh.

"I'm letting go, give it a try."

I start to slip, my toes turning outwards.

"Whoa." He catches me before my butt hits the ice.

Double whoa.

I'm wondering how much my dad is paying him. I hope it's enough.

"Maybe we should start with how to stand first. Hold on to my arms like this." He places my hands on his forearms.

"Feel secure now?"

A warm rush travels from my head into my stomach.

"Put your toes straight, bend your knees."

Wait, can you repeat that? I was busy counting your freckles.

He pushes his arms out, guiding mine along, and we're eagles ready for flight.

I'm the fledgling, and he's the master flier.

When he lets me go, I glide like I'm Nancy Kerrigan. Just kidding. But I'm upright and I have all my fingers.

Can you teach me more? I want to say to him when thirty minutes had passed. I will practice and practice if you are near.

My dad places a Jackson in my instructor's palm and shakes his hand.

"Thanks, man," he says, exiting the rink.

I never saw my instructor again.

I wish I knew his name.

TAXI, PLEASE
in the front seat
passenger side
that's where I want to ride
but it's the back row for me
because dad said so
and the requirement for that phrase

is the proverbial
why
and I continue to ask
why
and why
and please give proof until
one of us cracks
and I'm in need of
an upgrade, dad
first class never hurts
anybody in coach

nope
he points to the invisible
passenger beside him
it's not safe up here

the throne is high
and I'm likely to fall

but I'm almost fourteen
and—I left this part
out because
I think dad's ears might just
bleed—I became a woman
and isn't that enough
to get a ticket
to the front

you're not big enough
you don't weigh enough
if the airbag deploys
you won't withstand its force
if we're in an accident you could
fly through the windshield

don't sit in the middle
and are you buckled?

it's my freshman year
and the media is analyzing the crash
that took the People's Princess
in a tunnel
among the wreckage
of broken glass and twisted metal

you're in the back
until I say you're ready

and when will that be—
when I'm twenty-three?

if I ride in the front, I won't look
like dad is the chauffeur
in our four-door sedan
with a crank to roll
the window down
and mine's wide open
I'm nauseous from the stop-and-go
on Clove Road
next time, I'm walking
it's possible a turtle
could get to class faster
when a familiar car pulls alongside us
the driver waves
I slink down into my seat

my friend's father has a distinctive honk,
always in threes
and on the third honk
he holds the horn for a few seconds

to get the message
message received
dad leans over to roll down
the passenger window

what's going on, man?

just wanted to know, he pauses,
pointing to me in the back seat

you run a taxicab?

I guess SO,
my father's face grows red

see dad, I TOLD you so

my best friend laughs
from the passenger side
of a white Toyota
she knows I'm hiding
my face behind a backpack

hey, Jack
the driver announces
we'll get you in the front yet

that was the last day
I sat in the back

next up: child safety locks

LAMB STEW
I change my top
in a bathroom stall
because mom says:

you can't
show that kind of skin
at that kind of school

what kind of school?
I ask her

all the boys
and all their hands
and the priests
and nuns will be there

but I am
a lamb
and I do as lambs do
to please the ewe and so
I leave the house
without my shoulders in view
no worries, mom
the ewe sighs
her lamb
will not succumb
to the demands
of spring hands
while in her winter's wool

my new tank top has
spaghetti straps
with pink and gray stripes
and I remember
the drunken taciturn dreams
of pink elephants on parade
we dance in polka dots
in the gymnasium
the lions watch

the boys at the dance
the boy who asked me to dance
at the all-boys' school dance
lions come
and lions go
the lions circle around

a hand climbs up the stripes
rung by rung
and then back down
pink
gray
pink
gray
where the ladder rests
I protest
at the mothership launch
don't press the button
my button
I'll end up in stew
lamb stew
baked into the crust
a sorry ewe
mother will be

he holds his hands high
for me to see
and waves a good-bye
no shepherd,
little lost lamb
at a winter's dance
without your fleece
you will freeze

FOUR

YELLOW TAPE

YELLOW TAPE
I hold a cigarette
on the corner of Victory
and Clove Road
it isn't my own

Jack, she says,
hold this for me
but, Pat—

it's just for a sec, come on—
I gotta pee

she runs into the gas station
and strands me there
lit up
for all to see
is this what it feels like
to want nicotine?
maybe I could try it

but then there's cancer
your breath
your teeth
and worse of all,
there's your mother
your father
and they're not smiling
a slow-moving car
drives past the field
across the street
where an empty diamond
stains the grass
why is it that they
watch from afar?

hey uniform girl:
are you naughty?
are you nice?
please, don't think it over twice
if you want my advice
stick to ladies your own age
dirty old man
it's shriveling in my hand
it'll leave a mark
a permanent scar
how can I give a peace sign
ever again
like at mass
when I can't reach over
the pew
or I'm too damn lazy
to shake hands

that's a sign of an A and P Catholic,
Grandpa Ed once said,
the ones that come out for
ashes and palms

I crush Pat's stub
beneath my brown oxford—
oh no, it's still alive
it's going to burn
and I think about Smokey Bear
because I'm friends with the ducks
in Martling Lake
I can see them circle laps
as I stamp out the
flame
I've fed them
called them by name:
on duck (with the green feather)
on duck (with that strange red patch
over its eye)
and on, well, one is a swan
and sometimes the Canadian geese join—
to feast on crusts of
white bread and sometimes stale
Italian loaf hand-delivered
by dad and me
from a rowboat
he told me about the
time it sunk
and the reeds pulled
at his feet and

tried to swallow him
like my JanSport
when I carry Global Studies
the whole world is on my back
but I'm still rounding up to
five-foot-one

there's no way
they're letting us on

Pat lights up another
and blows a cloud of smoke
from the corner of her mouth
cooler than the sailor man
with the anchor on his bicep
that bulges
when he swallows a jar full of green
the light turns,
it's the S61
a chariot for the champions
from the ferry
its celebratory wheels go round
and round
and pass our stop

told ya,
my guide reassures me

it's packed like sardines

the pinstripe variety
a dozen or more
blue and white painted faces stare
eyeballs like a fish in a bowl
when my goldfish Cleo

is glued to his flakes—
the fresh flakes taste best
if they sit too long in the water
they sink

the exit door opens:
should I get on?
it's wrong not to pay the fare
and my MetroCard is free to me
a full-time student
from nine to three
I don't want to wait another
minute,
or it's a walking stick for me
1 foresee a date with a man
behind the screen
he works for the great and powerful

come on, get on

she nudges me forward
and there they were,
the sardines
out of the can
alive with ticker tape glory
glory, hallelujah
I find myself without Pat
she shrugs
and makes her way to the front
of the bus—
let me say, Pat
how much I admire you
for allowing me
to be your ashtray

———

I like your bag,
says a new friend
he sits on a blue seat
stationed near the window
and examines my side
zipper with the keychain
dangling:
FUR IS DEAD
an aroma
of another aluminum can floats
and burrows inside my nose

yeah, and I like your socks,
his friend adds
he wears a cap
on his head
an abbreviation of
the Big Apple
nice knees

my mind has
wheels it turns
and I must find a way to
get to the yellow tape
but I only have this pole to grip
and I'm feeling sick
the only girl left
in the back and I can feel their eyes
prodding me
drawing circles on my thighs
I'd like to thank the Sisters
for their distaste in pants
I hope it matters *if* and

when I'm found
and why is there
a red sneaker being passed around
surfs the crowd of blue and white
pinstripes grab the emergency
lift:

yo, bro—
open it, fast

and the window is wide open
alive with rounds of laughter
full mouth, I see your tonsils
laughter
for some guy is
going home
with one shoe on
and one shoe off
microwave brains
that must be the answer

what is your number?
I will call you, says the first boy,
his thumb and pinky out,
a surfer of the MTA
I shake my head
how about the dial tone—
can I ring my mom instead?

how old are you?
you look like maybe you're thirteen
the sardine brothers laugh

dude, if she can pee,
she's old enough for me

———

my admirer and his
jester like to stare at me
from head to toe
licking their lips
cats to a tuna can
there's nothing to stop
the cats when they want
to play
with retractable claws
and paws without mitts
their idols hold the glove
that fits

my eyes sting
and I'm not a bee
but I wish I had a stinger
and a loud buzz
no noise wants to leave my
caterpillar tongue
up above I see
a familiar overpass
it's the place I call home
get me home
yellow tape
yellow tape
yellow tape
follow the yellow tape

courage,
lion where are you
move your feet
it's only a stretch
above his head

and then you'll be back
better move before you
turn to cement
cement pours sticky at first
like the time
the gray goop filled
my grandparents' driveway
there were a few men
standing inches in
and my grandma said:
stay in the backyard
when your bathing suit is on
and don't talk to them
we don't know what's in their head

COME ON, JACK
think yellow tape
you can push it
yellow tape
a little bit closer
press it
yellow tape
the wheels have stopped
both of my ugly
brown shoes kiss the asphalt
on Bradley Avenue
but not before
my knight in pinstripes
declares

I love you
he screams
for the rest of Exit II to hear

———

you're my girl
his arms held wide open
from the emergency window

no thank you,
I'm allergic to seafood

BISTRO
you only want soup?

I only want soup,
I tell the boy
sitting across from me
with a passion for black shirts
and pants
and boots even though
it's ninety degrees
I place a napkin on my lap
because I am in the presence
of a white tablecloth
and I've been told
that fancy tablecloths and
cloth napkins require
proper attention
and nicer attire
don't wear jeans
mom and grandma
recommend
and thus (not *so*, because
so is not fancy)
my floral dress has a date

———

two beans jump
when I stir clockwise
insides splatter
the tablecloth
like at high tide
the surf
plays tag with the jetties
FYI:
don't walk on the jetties
you'll slip on the rock
hit your head
and it's lights out,
octopus garden

it's hard for me to eat
with butterflies
rumbling inside my ribcage
a boxing match with wings
but the more
I think about it
the more I realize
I'm completely mad
I chose the wrong
genus
if one paid attention
in fourth grade science class
it goes something like this:
kingdom
phylum
class
order
family

genus
species
and the trouble is
they're actually moths
because moths come out
at night
and they might be as mad as me
because I've let them go
hungry and
they threaten to return
to the surface

I am ready
to flee with them
grab a wing
and go
I'm thankful
that the dinner is shorter
than I expected
since I cut three courses
down to one
but his plate is full
the boy
with an appetite
for the summer night
he places the Styrofoam box
that holds his leftovers
on the last stair
by the railing

come here
he says, with the flick
of his finger

I inch a little closer
my wedges are higher
than I thought
and I don't want to look
like a wobbly fawn
he places his hands
at my waist
draws me
to his chest
and he kisses me
under the full moon
outside the bistro
he kisses me with his tongue
that I have never tasted before
it tingles and sends
the moths to the lamp
the streetlight flickers
in the parking lot where
two men
lean against a Cadillac
one calls out
when's the wedding?

he elbows the man next to him
and they laugh
I turn two shades of red
ripe tomato red
for I know they were watching
the whole time
they were watching while
I had my first kiss
and they don't know

my date doesn't know
only the moths and I know
I'm a little old
for a first kiss at sixteen
but I'm a good learner
and I want more practice
before the night is done
and then I will achieve
first base credentials
add them to my resume
I wonder if colleges would consider them
for extracurricular activities

I will add to my application essay:
she was kissed outside the bistro
she was kissed in clear view
of a Cadillac
she was kissed by a boy
all dressed in black
one she'd never see again
when the summer came to an end

GECKO
can you grab it?
can you catch it?

he flicks his tongue inside my mouth
like the gecko
at the pet store with
a palate for crickets
and I'm pretty confident that the gecko

is a better date—
he'd come to the door
scale the wall
ring the bell
so dashing in a little bow tie
and green suit
he presents me with
a bouquet of roses
possibly with a few leftover
wings but I will not judge
because he put in the effort and
listens as I speak
follows every word I say
without the need to play
games in a parking lot

I don't want to, I say
can we talk?

you're turning out worse than Willoughby
I should have stayed home
and watched Alan Rickman
rescue a crying Kate

his hand slips between my thighs
I push him off
he examines me
like I might
have another eye
growing in the center
of my forehead

you're too young
this ain't working

———

or maybe
I just want
to get to know you first
and the longer I stay
the more
I don't want to

The Nameless

I like Wednesday afternoons. Wednesday is payday, and the tips are great, too. I keep those in the pockets of the black apron that my godmother gave me—it's slick and shiny. I tie a knot in the back, and I feel like Catwoman as I shampoo clients at the sink and on occasion there's the guy who tells me a dirty joke and I'm supposed to smile and say:

"You're clever."

Smile, smile. Remember that smile.

"Would you like coffee?"

Sure, I can make a new pot. Sure, I just made one but if you insist.

"Cream and sugar?"

He opens his wallet, moves around a few green bills, and pulls out a dollar. He tucks it inside the pocket of my apron and gives it a pat for safekeeping. At least it's not change. I hate jingling.

"Thanks." But I don't get to escape without another joke. Super funny, once again. *Late Night* has an opening.

When I walk home from work, I hold my keys in the palm of my hand. I let one hang out to the side because I have a destination.

To whom it may concern, I have a destination. A simple fact of being a woman: taking a walk is never just taking a walk.

"Jackie," a voice calls out from behind me. I pause, my goosebumps at full salute. Did I imagine a strange voice in the wind? But the voice repeats my name, and a little louder this time, leaving no mistake of my senses.

It's not every day that a man announces my name. Like anywhere. Except for when I mistake my grandpa calling out to my grandma—I'm her namesake, so it's bound to happen from time to time—and we both answer, and he laughs and says, "No, I meant the bigger one." But after that, the only other men in my life are my dad and then there's my uncle who lives next door. It's too early in the day for either of them to be around, so I can only suspect that it's a serial killer. A psychopath. Like Mike Myers but it's not his season yet and he doesn't have conversations. He doesn't have to be a weird-looking dude, either. Sometimes they go around with handsome faces and compliments. Like Ted Bundy. Or maybe there's a motive. Someone sent to snuff me out—that's how it's said in the movies—and leave my remains somewhere where I'll never be discovered.

I've arrived at the top of my block. The stranger puts the SUV in park. If I talk to him through the window, then maybe he won't come out. If I run back home, will he follow? But I can't show fear. Sharks can smell fear. That's what the scuba divers report after every incident. They panic, they flap their arms about, and then— bam. Chunks of flesh. Not going to happen, I'm keeping my arm.

I take a step towards the window, leaving at least a foot between myself and the car door. He looks directly into my eyes. Don't look away, never look away. *Hold eye contact or you'll appear weak,* the self-defense instructor said on the evening news during a segment about protecting oneself as a woman while walking through the park. Or in a parking lot. Or when shopping. Or anytime I set my foot outside the house. And what happens to the weak in nature?

They get eaten. Not going to be a gazelle with an injured leg on the Serengeti.

"Jackie?" he repeats. "Hi."

How does he know me? Have I met him before? I stare back at him. I can't help it, but I feel a need to examine every aspect of his face. Draw a diagram: eyes, brown; hair, wavy; jawline, wide; neck, thick.

I wish I knew jiu-jitsu or had nunchucks or at least could throw a punch. Sadly, my physical expertise stops short of jump rope and hopscotch. Except for a little bit of Tae Bo, thanks to my enthusiastic (and severely disillusioned) high school gym teacher.

"Want a ride?" he asks, pointing to the empty passenger seat. The gray upholstery matches the exterior.

"No."

"You don't need a ride?"

"No."

"But aren't you hot?"

"Yes."

Wrong answer.

"So, you do need a ride."

Ugh. It's August and I'm dripping like a leaky faucet. If I survive, I'm writing to the maker of my so-called antiperspirant.

"I mean no. I don't need a ride."

Damn. Tripping over my words. Probably not the first reluctant hitchhiker.

"Come on, I'll take you wherever you want."

He looks about my uncle's age. Forty-something or so. My stomach decides that it no longer wants to be a participant in this conversation. But my curiosity is going to kill me faster than any cat out of nine lives.

"How do you know my name?" I ask. Because I don't know you. Let's not be friends.

He glances down at my V-neck.

Oh. Shit.

I had asked my father for a nameplate for my sixteenth birthday. All the girls in high school had one. All thanks to a Cosmopolitan-drinking, postcoital-smoking, sex columnist with a passion for untamable men, Carrie Bradshaw. Each week, teenage girls (and their moms, or whoever has HBO) tune in to imagine how they'd look in Manolos while sipping on cocktails. Carrie—who, by the way, somehow manages to afford rent in a ridiculously nice-size apartment in New York City in spite of her writer's salary and an addiction to eight-hundred-dollar pairs of shoes—attends boozy brunches and trendy nightclubs while wearing a necklace with the letters of her name looped in gold cursive. On my birthday, I opened a velvet cushioned case to find a 14-karat double gold-plated necklace with diamond accents hugging the curves of my name. I just *had* to have the necklace, and this is what I get for being a sheep. All that will be left is my name on a marble slab. I won't have time to write an epitaph, it would say:

She made it to the top of her block.

"I got to go."

"No. I'm going to take you home."

Should I run? But he'll come for me at night. He'll find me in my room with my little sister. And then there's my mom and my grandparents. I can't have him finding the whole family.

"I'm engaged," I lie. "My fiancé won't be happy about this."

"What do you mean? Where's your ring?"

I stare at my hand. It feels naked.

"He's saving up, it doesn't matter to me," I continue with my fictional tale.

"He's lucky. And you're too young for marriage." Advice coming from the man who could be my father. How fortunate I am to be in the presence of wisdom.

"So, no ride?" He grips the steering wheel.

"No ride, thank you." I wonder if the polite police are nearby.

"Here, take this if you change your mind."

He stretches his arm towards the passenger window. Between his thumb and forefinger is a small piece of paper. I snatch it from his hand like there's a small pair of pinchers attached. A name is scribbled: E———. And ten digits belonging to the man who refuses to take no for an answer. If thought bubbles could appear over my bewildered head at this particular moment, they'd say: Where does he store his secret stash of calling cards? In his pockets? Dashboard? Or is this a one-time thing, just for me?

"I'll come get you. Anytime. Anywhere."

"That's okay."

I cross over to the opposite side of the road and start walking towards a block with a high slope and a row of brick houses. I pretend that it's a stroll in the park and I have a picnic basket, and everything is just dandy, just grand. It's a sunny day in May and I'm like Daisy, that lady in that song who didn't want to give an answer to a creep on a bike who kept following her around the park. But I smile because I don't want to end up on *Unsolved Mysteries*.

I listen as the wheels pick up gravel and continue farther down the road. I glance over my shoulder. The gray SUV is standing at the traffic light. I wait until he makes a right turn before I retrace my steps and walk home.

The Errand

I stand on my tiptoes and lean my forearms over the counter. I must have missed the lunch rush, because I'm the only one in line at the pizzeria. Usually there's a line of customers waiting to sink their teeth into a slice, lap up a spoonful of pasta fagioli, or grab a meatball sub to go. I try not to drool as I stare at the display of garlic knots, calzones, fried zucchini sticks, and half a tray of sausage and broccoli rabe. That's just the first shelf. The row beneath is dedicated to more cheesy goodness: mozzarella sticks, fried ravioli, and rice balls. Even the rice balls have categories: cheese, spinach, parmigiana, and my favorite, the arancini. I can taste the Sicilian side dish just by looking at it—past the round layer of breadcrumb, parmesan cheese, and then there's the best part, the center, stuffed with beef, pork, and peas, and surrounded by mozzarella that stretches by the mile.

I lean in a little farther. Behind the counter is where the magic takes place. I allow my nose to remark on the combination of basil, tomato, and cheese wafting from a steel cage with grates. A round pie with sauce and fresh mozzarella sits on the rack. And just as I thought my afternoon couldn't get any better—lightning strikes. He's here.

The man who makes the magic. He holds the peel by its wooden handle, gliding the pie from the oven into a cardboard box where it will embark upon a new life. That is until some lucky customer bites into the crisp of its crust and reflects with an *ooh*, followed promptly by an *aah*, and then its whole delightful existence will be a sweet, savory memory.

The man with the superb arm for pizza maneuvers wipes his hands on a white apron tied to his waist. He catches me as I stare. I develop a sudden fascination with the parking lot outside the store window.

"Can I help you?" he asks, removing the apron.

In many, many ways. I hug the counter a little more.

"I'm here for the order," I manage to say without my usual fumble of words. Words that often lose their order and overall sense of purpose in the presence of savory food. Or the twenty-something-year-old in a white t-shirt and faded blue jeans.

"You work at the salon?" He points to the window. "That one across the street with the butterfly on the sign?"

"Yes. That's the one."

As a matter of fact, it's the only salon across the street. But I won't point this out. I find that when I make a point, I break the tip. Especially when I sharpen the point on my standard No. 2, the only pencil allowed to fill in the little bubbles on the Scantron answer sheets. Make your choice, they say, fill in a, b, c, d, or e, color them dark, and fill them in completely, no stray marks. No exam scheduled for today, but surely, I would pass.

Subject material, motivation: his skin has been touched by the sun. Classic olive. If I didn't need to use 50 ultraviolet block every time I walk outside, I'd have a bronze glow too. Like one of those goddesses who lie on the beach in July. They bring a towel, no chair. No umbrella.

"You're a shampoo girl?" he asks, questioning my entire existence up until this point with my errand for the afternoon.

"I'm a girl, and yes, I *work* with shampoo." And I'm an errand girl. I pick up the hair, I pick up the towels, and most of all, I pick up lunch.

He runs his fingers through his hair. Dark black and thick. Genetics are lucky for some. "I mean, you wash *heads*, right?"

Roman physique. Check. The kind that is chiseled into marble. Check. Fingers tap a beat. Check. That would be my own. Stop doing that. Say something:

"I wash the clients' *hair* before they get styled."

The pizza connoisseur rubs his chin. I think he's working on a secret pizza sauce formula. "How about next time you wash *me*?" He smiles with half a lip. He is saving the rest for later. Have a chance to walk my fingers through his hair? All that hair? That's a resounding yes from me. Hair like that requires a repeat shampoo. It's a necessity.

"Sure, call us." I mean me. Call me.

He takes a step closer to the counter. I can see the stubble growing in along his sideburns. Equally fantastic. "You look like that girl in that shampoo commercial. The one where she glistens in the sunlight." He brushes a loose strand of hair away from my eye.

I have to send a thank-you note to the manufacturer of my conditioner.

"You want a slice?" He winks. I really don't know how I managed it, but I caught one this time. Too bad it's a catch-and-release kind of day.

"The order's fine, thanks." I grab the paper bag lined with grease from the counter. I flip my hair over my shoulder and watch him watch me leave.

Sometimes, I'm an errand girl. Sometimes, all I want is lunch.

The Crossing Guard

I unbuckle my belt. I am a woman on a mission.

"Stop the car, Mom!"

"What now?"

My mother is not pleased with me: I may or may not have told her last-minute that I need ink for the printer.

"There's a turtle!"

"What? Where?"

"There's a turtle in the middle of the road." I point to the double yellow lines.

"I have to save her—she's not going to make it." I gather my cape—just need to settle on a color—perhaps dusty rose? Olive green? Earth tones are usually the best choice for brunettes. Or at least that's what I read once in *Marie Claire*. Or was it *Cosmo*? As long as it flaps over my shoulders in a dramatic flowing motion, I'll be satisfied.

"Go now," she says. Mom is allowed to take as many verbal liberties as she pleases, not only because I was once an occupant of her womb but because she is now the commander of Operation Save the Turtle.

"While the light is red." She annunciates the *r* in *red* like she's revving up the engine on a cold winter morning. And it's most advantageous to warm up before physical exertion.

Stretch it out, ladies. That's what my physical education instructor used to say before she sent us to run laps around the gymnasium. Maybe I should have listened and not taken more than five minutes to tie my laces. Pesky buggers, I had no choice but to retie them a few minutes later. But to save the turtle, I must forgo such necessities.

"You're in a pickle," I whisper to the terrapin, bending over to inspect her. Lucky gal. She manages to escape without a single scratch, and I can't last a single day without smudging my French manicure. Horns blare in my direction. I look over my shoulder to discover—to my horror—the light has turned green. In the words of Mr. Presley, turtle dear, *it's now or never.*

"Hurry, the light, the light!" the commander waves her hand out the window. Apparently, there's more than a few motorists expressing their dismay over a girl playing crossing guard on Martling Avenue.

I pick up the jaywalker from the back of her shell. She has a beak that looks as if it could snap off the tips of my fingers. I dash across the double lines. Not amused by my valiancy, her mouth opens wide—if I spoke reptilian, I'm sure I'd get an earful worse than the one I'm going to get later about being organized. And responsible things like checking on ink levels.

See here, turtle friend. My mom says that sometimes I'm a real testaruda. *And I learned that in Italian that means headstrong, but aren't you glad that I am, you'll be safe because I'm a real* testaruda. *It all makes perfect sense.*

I make it to the curb and run towards the park.

If you needed a ride, we would have known had you grabbed yourself a pole. Any old stick would have sufficed—plenty of those in Brooks

Pond—and tied a red handkerchief around it, stuck out your foot, and voilà, a bona fide reptilian hitchhiker. Just ask Frog and Toad.

I call a truce when we reach the edge of a pond with green moss.

My mother passes me a bottle of antibacterial gel from her purse. "Don't touch your face, salmonella!"

I don't want to brag, but I'm sort of a turtle superhero.

Don't Tell Grandma

It's not Sunday dinner. It's Tuesday and I should be depressed because it's one of those days of the week that involves school and work and other bullshit that does not include late night movie binges or sleeping in. Or meatballs and fusilli and ricotta. But I'm not sad. Want to know why? Because of chicken cutlets. When it's chicken cutlet night, I'll go for another helping of the crispier pieces. I like them a little burnt and I love them right out of the skillet. And since I'm a grandma's girl—there's no reason to deny it—I snag the best piece right out of the oil without a moment to absorb on the paper towel lining the casserole dish.

"I'll have more mashed potatoes," I said, as grandma fills my plate with a second helping. She slides the butter dish in my direction. The woman is a mind reader.

"Do you want beets?" Grandpa holds up a bowl of round red slices swimming in their own beet juice. "They're good for your blood," he insists.

"No, I'm good, Poppy." Beets aren't my thing. They stain the tablecloth and then grandma spot-cleans it with a *mopina* (that's a dishcloth) and a drop of blue dish detergent. We use the brand that helps with removing oil from the feathers of those poor ducks caught in spills. Works wonders on beet stains and sauce stains. And as a woman, I can tell you it works miracles on monthly inconvenience stains. But don't bring that up at the table unless you want to start a riot.

"How about the spinach?" grandma asks.

"Okay, just a little." Spinach is good for you, I know it is, but why is it always so spinach-y? Green and limp and just there.

"You need a little green," my great-grandma insists. She adds more butter to her slice of Italian bread.

"I'll have some," I say, shoveling a forkful into my mouth. And here, at this very table, as I sit across from my mother and sister, who, by the way, have more protein and carbohydrates on their plates than the green leaves that bunnies like to consume—and I'll never ever understand why Peter Cottontail would risk losing more than his good coat and his mother's contentment and miss out on dessert all because of leafy plants—something amazing happens inside my mouth. The spinach is no longer spinach. It's actually—don't get mad at this, grandma—it's really tasty. What is this kitchen sorcery?

"Is this the same spinach?" I ask her, as she pours orange juice into her glass.

"Same as I remember. Out of the bag as usual."

"Not a different brand?"

"Nope, the same."

It doesn't make sense, but hey, it's good for me and I'll have some more. Who knows, maybe I'll grow another inch. But doubtful, since I'm eighteen and female. When it's over, it's over, step stools for life.

"There's no more water," my sister announces. Mom grabs the empty pitcher and stands up.

"Stay and eat," grandma tells my mother. "I'll get it."

I feel a nudge at my elbow. Great-grandma leans over and whispers in my ear, "It's the salt."

"The salt?" I answer, my mouth full of greens. She points to the pot on the stove. Then shakes an imaginary bottle in the air.

"Oh, the salt," I say, watching as grandma drops ice cubes into the pitcher.

"Shh," the matriarch holds a finger to her lips. I zip my lips with an imaginary key. I throw the key at the bowl of beets. What grandma doesn't know won't hurt her.

FIVE

TWITTERPATTED

The Roof Man

A ladder leans against a blue ranch with purple shutters. Yes, purple shutters. My grandmother's favorite color. On top of the roof, there is a man. He wipes the sweat from his face with a red bandana.

Roof Man: Do you make a habit of making out with strangers in the street?

Me: If you mean my boyfriend, then yes.

Roof Man: What's his name?

Me: Why do you want to know?

Roof Man: My name is better.

The Mundane Sundae

"I don't like how he sits in my armchair reading our newspaper. And crosses his leg, like he's a king."

Grandma's hands are folded in her lap. She's seated on the couch in the living room. There's only one thing to know about the lavender couch with a floral motif in my grandparents' ranch: it's the epicenter of family life. On Thanksgiving, it holds the overflow of grandchildren with their turkey dinners set on folding tables. At Christmas Eve, it seats anxious little guests waiting to greet Santa and ogle the stockpile of gifts with red trimmings. On Easter Day, it hides fluorescent eggs filled with jellybeans as rabbit enthusiasts follow baby powder bunny tracks down the hallway. And on special occasions such as tonight, when the eldest granddaughter brings over a gentleman caller (yep, that's the label), it serves as a lecture hall.

I've joined her on the couch. Her eyebrows are in the raised position, and I know there's a serious talk brewing. And it's all his fault. Who comes into someone's house and doesn't talk? Opens up the paper, sticks his nose between the pages, and doesn't say a word—*rude,* that's the word she used as soon as he left. I mean, my grandma isn't wrong—is the *Staten Island Advance* better company than me?

"He's no good for you—too comfortable, too quick. I don't like him. And I don't like his ways." She waves her hand across her face like she's shooing a fly.

"Yes, Grandma." I reply, trying to avoid eye contact. Stare too long and she'll pull the truth right out of me. I'm not about to tell her that it's really about his six-pack abdominals. Or that I plan on keeping him for a little bit longer, because the boyfriend title is new to me and I like to say it out loud.

"You should keep your options open."

"Open?"

"Yes, open."

Options. I'm not good with them. When standing on line, waiting to order an Italian ice, I find I can't decide:

Cherry

Chocolate

Cotton candy

Lemon

Watermelon

One hundred other flavors

There's also an entirely different list of cream ices—and I can dream in gelato. Oh, but then I could miss out on an ice cream sundae. Or a banana split. Or a root beer float. And what if I'm stuck with chocolate? Only chocolate ice cream for the rest of the afternoon, wasting my taste buds—I'll get a case of the mundane sundae blues.

And they have smoothies now, too. "It's too much," I tell my grandma. It's all too much.

A month passed. The door, wide open.

THE CLOTHESLINE

periwinkles dance in June
when I put on my sundress
with a sweetheart design
I like to wear a garden
in my hair
a wreath of scattered branches
by the umbrella line
where grandma keeps her secret stash
of clothespins in a muslin bag
gray and white stripes
faded by the afternoon light

I fasten a pair of wooden legs
to the plastic cable lines
the four-corner post
a metal pole at the center
decorated in green to find
two triangles play tag
with string ties
I turn my bikini bottom
upside down
and attach a clothespin
to the left
and then to the right
my hips declare
I am a pear

pears are sweet
but I prefer a peach
and the way the juice
dribbles down my chin and when
I taste it I dream of salt water

in my hair and a picnic on the
beach
sand beneath my feet
I stop to listen to
the sound of the surf
as it breaks on the shore
when I discover
I am not alone

hello
a voice calls to me—
the tide recedes and
the peach disappears

hello there
somewhere the wind
desires my ear
and I am unaware
that the clothesline has reception
who is there?
and why the need to shout
no echoes to spare
this isn't a castle
no abandoned hall
no rooms with
couches covered in cloth
no film of dust
no secrets stalking the attic—
if I had an attic
there would be paperbacks
and a few hardcovers

HEY, GIRLY
I do not believe the spirit converses

in cat's tongue
with my hand at salute
I shield my eyes
from the sun's high beams
and discover
a man waving from his deck
with a spatula in hand,
flipping carnage
on an open grill

me?
I point to myself
I am armed
with wooden pins

girl, with the clothes
the spatula
is pointing towards me
and I cannot deny
for I am
holding a pair
of short-shorts my mother despises
the smoke clouds his face
turns red to match
the top
of his bald head

hi
I hang the impetuous shorts
they are not short enough
to end
this conversation

I like how you hang your clothes
he says,

sweat dripping from his brow

thanks
I give a gracious smile,
as a recipient of the
clothesline award
I would make a speech
but I come unprepared

is there room for mine too?
he flips so that the summer sausage is even
on both sides

room?
the shorts have a hanging thread
I wonder if the pair of scissors
in the bathroom drawer
are handy

for my clothes
he winks,
but the garden is wilting
and the periwinkles need watering

sorry
I address the man
with the stainless steel
utensil—
line's all full!

PHARMACY 101: AISLE 5
late night run
to a twenty-four-hour pharmacy: aisle 5
is where I find

shampoo for curly hair
a bottle of elixir
to tame
a stubborn mane

find what you need?

aisle 5 supplies
a boy
in a blue polo shirt
with a nametag
grabs the bottle
from my hand

cute kangaroo,
he says, examining my latest
hair care craze

I like the commercials
with the kangaroo that—

that winks?

the pharmacy boy with
almond brown eyes
returns the bottle
and folds
his fingers over mine

that's, uh,
the one

smooth, real
smooth
a bit of volume
would do me
some—

———

good stuff?

I think so

aisle 5 is alive with
magic beans

need anything else?

he flashes me a smile
and I want to applaud him
for his dimples
but I can't act
like I'm from the discounted bin
with a twenty percent after summer
sale sticker
might as well
stamp it
smack in the middle
of my forehead

I could use something
to hold the—

don't do it
hold it in
don't—
but I did
let out a giggle
a schoolgirl laugh
that happens
every time I'm nervous

what?

———

the bounce in my curls

he knows
Christ, he knows
he put my tongue in a knot
and I believe—oh, yes
I see it there, he's curled
his lip to the side—
enjoying my stumble

you should try this
he points to a bottle
of green liquid

aisle 5
has a cauldron?

it sits
in the middle of a fiesta
of bright pink and purple
bottles
some silver
a few black
some are short
others tower over
and narrowly
miss the top of the shelf
bottles highlighted by
volume:
finish hold
flexible hold
freeze hold
and the ultimate

maximum full volume hold—
fighting
for first place

it's good for curls—
here, feel mine.

what?

I use it.

oh.

it's okay, you can touch it.

aisle 5
catches fire

your hair?

yes.

he slides his fingers
between my own
his thumb wrapped
around
like a steeple
but there's no church
and no other people
he releases my hand
to fit
on the top
of his head

it has a good hold.

so, we're sold?

———

I'm a satisfied customer.

got a pen?
he asks, scribbling in the air
with his finger

aisle 5
has a plan

I fumble in my denim bag
next to a crumpled tissue
and an empty gum wrapper
is an approved
black round

write your number,
he rips a coupon from
a red kiosk
I flip it
to the blank side

I'm gonna call you—
to check on the gel.

just in case I can't read the directions?

exactly.

exiting the twenty-four-hour pharmacy:

wait, what's your name?

aisle 5
delivers

PHARMACY 101: DO YOU HAVE AN OX?

A phone call with the pharmacy boy about the Oregon
    Trail:

Boy: I think I'm gonna lose—
my sister thinks I'm gonna lose.
Me: Why?
Boy: I'm at a river. Now what?
Me: What's your occupation?
Boy: Farmer.
Me: Do you have an ox?
Boy: No, mine died.
Me: That's not good.
Boy: Yeah, and I have some sort of disease.
Me: Dysentery?
Boy: That's the one.
Me: That's not good either.
Boy: What is that?
Me: You die from severe diarrhea.
Boy: Wow, you're smart.
Me: I know from playing so many times in computer
    class—that's all we did.
Boy: How do I win?
Me: Choose to be a doctor and you'll have money for
    supplies.
Boy: Oh, man.
Me: Sorry, try fording the river.
Boy: Shit, I died!

Pharmacy 101: Twitterpatted

PART I: IN THE CAR WITH TRAVOLTA

"You can't smoke that," I tell the pharmacy boy with a tattoo of another boy etched on his forearm. The boy is peeing. He is accompanied by an orange tiger with black stripes that is also peeing. They are comparing the size of their puddles.

"Nah, it's not that bad." He waves a cloud of smoke from his face. It lingers and adds to the growing fog in the car.

"My mom will smell it. She partied in the seventies, you know, the *Staying Alive* era. And she will recognize the smell—the skunk kind."

And not the cute one from *Bambi,* who gets twitterpatted. Damn it, I think I'm twitterpatted.

"I look like him," my date proposes.

He points his finger to the corner of the ceiling and brings it back to his chest and then back again to the corner of the ceiling.

"Travolta?"

Mr. Confident flashes a grin in the rearview mirror and then turns to me.

"Yeah, you wish."

He leans in. We play a game of catch and roll. I wonder if tongues are like mattresses, can they remember the shape?

"Come on, I'll let you drive." He dangles a set of keys. Attached to the ring of his keychain is a red discount card from the pharmacy. The more you use it, the better the points.

I shake my head.

"You should have a license already."

"I'm taking my time."

"Yeah, you're that kind of girl."

"What's that supposed to mean?"

"Like a good girl kind."

"Oh."

"Why else would I make out with you in my car and not on the street?"

"If so, come back to my house," I demand.

"Is anyone home?"

"Just my grandpa."

"Shit, I have to meet your grandpa?"

"It's only my poppy."

"What am I gonna say?"

"Talk to him about the Yankees. He loves them."

"What about you?"

"I've decided I'm not a baseball fan."

PART II: IN THE BASEMENT WITH GHOSTS

the Queen Anne sofa
and I,
and a boy who stocks
shelves in the twenty-four-hour pharmacy
share in the luxurious accommodations
of the basement

I turn the switch knob of a lamp
to illuminate the charm:
the living room is a private
lair with a bonus
built-in bookcase
the books are resting
while I explore
a non-fictional character
and this one happens to be
from the same century
as me

did you hear that?
he asks, hand cupped to his ear

no.

footsteps on the stairs?

my date's eyes are growing round
and rounder
and, I checked,
still red

oh, that's just ghosts.

ha. ha.

no really, the basement is haunted.

stop—maybe it's your grandpa.

if younger me
could see the grown up me
with a boy
and his tiger tattoo
his arm around me

fingers dangling
I imagine she'd wonder
why all the fuss
and she'd just go back
and take a book off the
shelf and find herself
settled on mom's Queen Anne—
a blue sofa with
climbing vines of pink and mauve bouquets—
it appears that a characteristic
of my matrilineage is a strict adherence
to floral patterns on upholstery—
in the same spot where
I read
an entire series
about a group of girls
who made a living
watching other people's children
my favorite
was a boy-crazy girl named Stacey McGill
and her summer observing
a New Jersey lifeguard

that's not his footstep. his is heavier.

I can't.
he moves his arm off my shoulder.

you can't?

how am I going to kiss you—and stuff—
with your grandpa upstairs?

it's not a big deal, he won't—

he's like a veteran or something, right?

———

a Korean War veteran.

that's some serious shit.

I would say so.

I'm going.

who's the goodie now?

I'm not, I got to go.

PART III: SIDEWALK OF GOOD-BYES

"Are you really going?" I follow him to the driveway.

"Yes," he says, searching the pocket of his jeans for keys.

"Why?"

"Because I can't just do *things,* with him in there."

"Okay, I'll see you on aisle 5 someday."

"Yeah, girl."

He pats his hair. I twirl mine. I like it when he wears his leather jacket. I grab a pocket and pull him towards me. We make memories on the sidewalk.

"You're killing me," I tell him.

"No, *you're* killing me."

He makes an X with his forefingers and holds them up to my face. "I'm going, Jack."

A car door slams.

He just can't.

A Party in Port Richmond

PART I: THE TALL BOY

I'm standing under an archway. The room on my right has a bar. The bar is lined with red plastic cups. The partygoers love their red cups so much that they help themselves to one cup after the next and the one after that and another one too. Repeat. After the red cups go empty, some of the party participants will be gracious enough to dispose of the plastic remainders into the wastebasket provided by the host. That would be the black garbage bag tied to the side of the bar by an umbrella rack. Sans the umbrellas. I'm going to make a wild assumption here and guess this party was not, in fact, organized by an actual adult. Like the kind who pays the mortgage.

As for the rest of the partygoers, they decide it's not worth the effort and discard their empty beverages on the countertop, the coffee table, the floor, in the cushions of the couch—and yikes, what a couch, not a floral motif to be found, and it's, *le gasp,* brown—and virtually anywhere the eye will turn, it will be blessed by red cups here, there, and everywhere. A bonus for the poor souls who are left to clean up after the presumed guests find themselves stumbling out, or until the alcohol is all gone, they will be greeted by an overflowing pathetic excuse for a receptacle that has managed to make matters much worse by ripping and spilling sticky beverage concoctions all over the wood floor.

It's a pity, because the flooring looks ancient and I'm pretty sure it's the real kind, with dark knots. I hope the cocktails—and Lord knows if they could actually be considered cocktails when the bartender looks as if he is barely old enough to drive—are worth ruining the pine.

The red cup cocktails are concocted in the two stool bar next to the basement stairs. There's a closet beneath the stairs that could easily fit a burgeoning wizard. The wizard would not have spilled the cocktails. Nor are the cocktails served by a bartender with a flashy smile who tosses bottles of happy juice in the air. But there's a boy I know from elementary school, sitting on the wicker stool, laughing with a guy who is rubbing his bald head. If he rubs hard enough, I wonder, will he be granted three wishes?

I wish I was home. The lighting sucks—old recess lightbulbs big and round and bug-eyed, staring at the party hoppers from the ceiling and giving everyone a yellow halo—like the glowworm doll I had when I was five. It's sort of like a bad 1970s sitcom down here, and worst of all, there aren't any windows. So that's a big fat NO.

The room to my left, I think it's a den. It's a place where the lady of the house banishes her loudmouthed older-than-teenage children who are not monetarily equipped to live on their own. Or where the husband escapes the nagging of his wife and turns on the TV with his hand in his pants on the couch. And, of course, a prime location for parties thrown by the habitants of the house who do not pay the water or the gas bill on a night when the taxpayers are out of town.

Surrounding the couch are folding chairs. Standard brown like the ones kept in the church basement to accommodate the overflow of parishioners who only show up for Christmas or Easter mass, and the poor souls pay in penance, because when they sit down, they'll discover that their backside has gone numb and tingly. The folding chairs are displayed in a horseshoe. The sitters are in conversation, two by two. Paired off by interest, paired off by level of attractiveness, the stragglers are left to stand.

Which leads me to this wall. To this archway, where I may be the Mary Bennet of the room. I hate that Mary gets so much crap for wanting to stay home and read her books. Getting dragged to fancy rich people balls so her more physically appealing sisters can play coy to potential husbands. And the one time she dares to participate—not much of a singer but the girl can play a concerto like nobody's business—she's ridiculed and blamed for scaring off eligible bachelors. Sisters. Forever preventing the other from being the shiniest star.

"Are you holding up the wall?" says a tall boy.

I lift my chin to respond. Otherwise, I'm just talking to a navel.

"There's too many people in there." I've seen him before. He's a server at the local diner. I know this because I may or may not have memorized his schedule.

"Let me know if you move. Can't have the wall cave in." He has the longest fingers. I bet his hand is twice the size of mine.

"Thanks, you'll be the first to know."

What??? That. Was. My. Watermelon. To think of the hours that I spent watching *Dirty Dancing* because it's always on TV. And I really hate the edited version—why take out all the juicy bits? Somehow, primetime can't handle a bit of extra skin when everyone knows that it's the best part of the movie, like the icing on the cake. But all that time, all that precious time wasted cringing as Baby informs the swoon-worthy Johnny Castle that she did indeed carry a watermelon to an underground hip-swinging, bodies-grinding, don't-bring-your-mom-to kind of party—all for nothing. None of my cinematic wisdom matters, anyhow, he left me alone with proverbial fruit to sit next to a girl who followed at his heels the entire night. He'll sit there with his hand on her knee and let that girl ramble on.

Good Lord. Call the convent. I give up.

"Guess what? Guess what?" Standing before me with a red cup in her hand is the girl who invited me—her neighborhood buddy is cousins with the host, who relies on umbrella stands to tether garbage bags. We met in Theology 101 as we tried to keep a straight face when the professor, Father Peter or Paul something, rambled on about how delightful it was to see women dressed in skirts on spring days. Blooming flowers, that's us. A bunch of blooming rose buds.

"What? What?" I answered, hoping that she'll surprise me by driving me home early.

She is cheery-eyed and cherry-cheeked.

"I know someone here who really wants to meet you."

I thought being in college would make me more mature and I would be discussing something sophisticated that requires me to drop the names of dead authors and poets and whip out my new-found knowledge of Walden. But no. I'm getting messages from a boy delivered by my friend, and it's as good as passing a note in sixth grade class. One of those origami folded notes with the corners tucked in so neatly that once I open it, I'll never be able to get it back the same way.

"I don't know, who?" I raise my shoulders in question. I imagine the guests as characters on flip style card holders from the *Guess Who?* gameboard that's gathering dust in my closet. Does he wear glasses? That's always a good question to ask when playing because if the character is nearsighted, ninety percent of the board will need to be flipped down and it guarantees a win.

Please say it's the tall boy. Has he said anything about me? I thought we had a connection by the pretzel bowl.

He said: "Try the dip, it's good."

To which I said: "It is."

But it was the smile and the eye contact that said it all, really.

"Just guess already," she says, placing her hands on her hips.

"How about that guy?" I point to a dude wearing a tight white t-shirt. His biceps are in desperate need of freedom.

"Be serious."

The Adonis is chatting it up with Miss Popular sorority chick, who is wearing a v-neck sweater with a plunge that is deeper than the bottom of the Pacific Ocean. Or is it the Atlantic? Doesn't matter, special submarines would be required.

"Then who?" I ask, wondering if I should have worn my push-up bra. I hate underwire, it's like a prison for boobs.

"See that guy over there?"

She points to two college guys conversing near the back door. A good basement has a reliable exit. Preferably a separate door from the main house, in respect for all transgressions. Venial transgressions may use the front entrance.

"So, is he the blond or the brunet?"

"The dark-haired one."

Not bad, another tall boy. Not as tall but he'll do.

I'll say my good-byes to Mary Bennet.

PART II: THE SAD BOY

We sit on the curb. He chooses a spot at the corner of the block where we'd have a little privacy. A crowd of basement dwellers have emerged and take refuge on the front lawn. Cigarette buds line the sidewalk and a trail of red cups pile on the stoop. Neighbors poke their noses through the blinds. A few have flashed their porch lights. It's only a matter of time before somebody calls in a 311. And I hope it happens soon, because the silence between us is growing louder than the cat outside my bedroom window that insists on calling for company at two a.m.

The moon is full, and I'm certain there's a few more craters I've never noticed. The tall boy has a cowlick that refuses to cooperate. He swats it away from his brow and attempts (and reattempts) to tame it into position with the rest of his wavy locks. He tells me I'm pretty as he tosses his cigarette in the sewer grate, but more so, I look like a nice girl, one who's easy to talk to. "Like, a good listener," he says.

I try to live up to my potential but it's hard to ignore the aroma of beer mixed with stale smoke and a hint of shaving cream. Reminds me of the can that my grandpa keeps underneath the bathroom sink, with a red stripe wrapped around it like the swirl on a peppermint cane. Wonder if he notices that it's lighter than it should be—surprisingly, it makes my legs shiny and smooth.

"Is it okay if I tell you some stuff?" He inches closer to me, our legs touching.

"Of course," I tell the boy I met minutes earlier. Maybe I'm his confessional for the evening. What could he possibly share that requires a nice girl with a good pair of ears?

"It's about my mom."

When it comes to moms, I know better than to get involved. Especially if the mom is the mother of a perspective future boyfriend.

"But I don't know your—"

"She's dead."

"I'm sorry. How did—"

"Cancer. Fuck cancer."

"Fuck it."

Last year, he says. Last year she left him. She wasted away in a hospital and left him in charge of his younger brothers. And his father.

"Know the worst part?"

I don't know if there is a part worse than losing your mother.

"Tell me," I squeeze his hand.

"The funeral parlor. I hated that place. Everybody telling me how sorry they were. That she's in a better place. How's dead a better place? How? And to see her lying there not looking like her, not looking like the mom we knew. How she made us whatever we wanted, and we can eat, all of us. Brought us to wherever we wanted to go, she was our taxi."

He cradles his arms around his knees, resting his head.

"And then the holidays, not the holidays anymore. Not to me."

I rub his shoulder. "I'm sorry." I have no words of use to fill a hole in a heart the way only a mom can. I have the urge to hug my mom. And my grandma. And my great-grandma. And my god-mother. They all need a hug.

"I miss her. I miss her around the house. And then there's my father. He's not the same. It's like he left himself somewhere. Somewhere with her."

It's not often I see men cry. I don't think they often see other men cry too.

He wipes the corner of his eyes with the back of his hand. "I want to know you, and now you only know about me." He turns to me, his eyes glassy.

"Talk all you need." I wipe a tear from his cheek. He takes my hand and brings it to his lips.

"I like you." He reaches his arm around me. I'm not a prude anymore but I still get a nervous jolt in my stomach right before a kiss. Like how much tongue is too much? What if I'm bad? What if he's bad?

He parts my lips and swirls inside my mouth. I'm surprised to discover that he is better than the last two boys I sampled. I return the favor.

We sit in silence, his arm still around me.

"Can I call you sometime?" He reaches into his back pocket and flips open his phone. I enter my digits into his contacts.

"This is your home phone?"

"Yes."

"No cell, huh?"

"No. No need for that nonsense." (I'm also broke.)

"I like you even more."

I leave him at the curb, wondering what I will say if he calls. I hope that he won't, and I can avoid the inevitable awkwardness that will follow my rejection. I'll lie of course. Make up some excuse of not being ready for a commitment. No, maybe I'll say I'm not over an ex-boyfriend. How can I tell the boy who poured his heart out to me, ripped it from his very sleeve, that the girl who wiped his tears and let him kiss her is a liar? A liar who pines over the taller boy in the basement.

PART III: THE BAD BOY

An older gentleman from across the street stands on his porch with his arms crossed. A peculiar taste in fashion, his undershirt rides inches above his waist, freeing his belly to poke above his pajama pants. Nothing kills a party faster than a pair of flannel pajama pants on the front porch.

"Let's go," my friend says, jingling her keys. I'm happy to go and I'll be even happier if I can avoid any eye contact with my curbside paramour.

"So, was he any good? Saw you guys out there, looking pretty cozy." She winks at me.

"Okay, I guess." I shrug my shoulders. Why bother telling the truth? I find that lying makes me feel shorter. If I lie any more, I'll shrink. And then I'll be forced to bite into a mushroom to return to all sixty-one inches of me, a nice girl with listening ears.

We walk down the block, because parking is an absolute nightmare and thankfully my friend can parallel park. I pretended that my car was in need of repair, so I didn't have to deal with the embarrassment of leaving a foot between my Chevy and the curb.

"Hey." Someone taps me on the shoulder. *Don't be you, please don't be you.* I can't face him again not knowing if I'll be able to look him in the eye. Me and my weakness for boys with bleeding hearts.

Saved by the blond boy from the basement. He is more my type with blue eyes and a sprinkling of freckles. Except for one trifling problem.

"Come around the corner with me." He gestures with his head.

"Why?"

"Because I want to taste you."

I remember an illustration of a red fox. He is licking his lips outside a wooden hutch lined with wire. "But I was just with your friend." Oh indeed, he is not just any old friend but the best friend of my sad boy.

"And?"

"Did you see us?"

"It's cool. We like to share."

"Not that kind of sharing."

"Come on." He grabs my hand.

"No." I pull away.

"It's not like we haven't shared before," he says, his eyebrows raised.

Silly me.

"Nah." I feel taller already.

"Phhhff," he mumbles.

Guess the fairy tales are true. A wolf in sheep clothing. A fox in the henhouse outsmarting the less-than-clever chickens. Does that make me some sort of naïve hen? Call me feathered.

It's a good thing I'm not in charge of any livestock.

The Boy with the Visor

"It's the weekend, you can't do homework on the weekend," says a girl from my Foundations of Education class. We are headed to the café on campus to grab an overpriced cup of Twinings. Black tea, low-fat milk, and two sugars. With a side of syllabus.

"I know, but I really should get a head start," I say, stirring in my sugar. She's trying to convince me to join her group of friends to see a movie. What she doesn't know is that I'm also planning to watch *Jane Eyre* for the millionth time. Mr. Rochester versus a bunch of people I've never met? Not really a contest.

"You're seriously going to waste a Friday doing an assignment that's not even due for what—a week?"

A month, if she wants to be technical. But I like to keep my GPA at a shiny 4.0. It's not unusual to find me after class at the library. There's this one spot on the second floor by the back windows that face Howard Avenue, that if I sit at the right angle, there's a great view of the bridge. When that doesn't work, I still have the view of the Wagner College track team as they make their way up the incline. Sans shirts. And I'm not one to complain.

"Just come see the movie."

"But I don't know Star Wars."

"You'll figure it out."

Episode II or something, *Clones* or something, all I know is that the only way I got through *A New Hope* and *Empire Strikes Back* was because of Harrison Ford, and this isn't *Indiana Jones* or *Working Girl* or *Sabrina*. Can't blame a girl for loving Linus Larrabee. But my friend has a point, how annoying.

So, I, being the brave little toaster that I am (ha ha), give in and join the merry band of friends I've never met. I try my hardest to avoid any trivia-related questions and just go with my general knowledge—the foot soldiers in the white getup are the bad dudes and so are the ones with the red lightsabers. I just discovered that it's lightsa*b*ers not lightsa*v*ers, but at least I got a good laugh as we wait for her friends to pick us up on the side of Victory Boulevard near the Blockbuster where I still have an overdue movie. I really should pay that off because I need another supply of malted milk balls and red vines and some sour patches, too—only watermelon though, I'm not fond of the lime or the lemon, not even crazy about cherry.

A sedan pulls alongside the curb as I contemplate what I'm going to order when we get there. It's a toss-up between chocolate-covered raisins (the healthier option) or gummy bears. Maybe I'll get both, live a little.

"You can squeeze in," the driver says, smiling at me. His girlfriend, sitting shotgun, waves at me. We were both in the glee club at high school. (Don't ask me to sing again, like, ever, it was strictly a college resume kind of activity.) Go figure. Only on Staten Island are there less than three degrees of separation. You usually know someone by their:

    a) family

    b) friend

    c) next door neighbor's cousin

"Sure," I say, because it's not like I have another option. Say no, then I'm considered rude or worse, I'm a priss who requires special handling. But why, really, why am I always in the back seat?

And of course, my luck, there's one spot left. Next to a boy wearing a blue visor. This boy has been eye-stalking me since his buddy put the car in park. Nothing at all like my tall boy (don't even ask) and nothing like the last guy I went out with, who just happened to help himself to my godmother's chocolate-covered strawberries. Although this may sound ridiculous, it is important to note that he never met my family before, only said hi, and then just walked over to my aunt's dining room table, reached over the display of desserts, and shoved one into his mouth.

So maybe the visor is not that bad? I don't know, because the visor is turned backwards with the strap across his forehead. What's with the backward look? Isn't the whole point to stop the sun from getting in your eyes? And it's nighttime, so why use it as an accessory at all? I think it would be odd of me—especially since I don't even know his name—if I pull the visor forward or just take it off of his head and rescue him from making any more fashion blunders.

I can tell he's interested because he keeps staring. And I know he's asking about me—and in the most obvious way too—he taps the shoulder of the former glee club member, and she shields her mouth with the side of her hand, so I can never guess what she may be saying.

I'm afraid this will be a long night, but I will reward myself with a tub of popcorn and add extra yellow stuff that's supposed to taste like butter. No worries, I'll eat it anyway, I reassure myself as I climb into the back seat next to the boy with the visor.

Note from the narrator: The boy with the visor no longer owns the blue visor or any other visor. There's not enough room in our closet.

SIX

WALL ART

THE ARBOR

we'll sketch the trees
the professor instructs
as we walk down Eddy Street
pass the row of Tudors
and circular driveways
I join
the front of the line
and dedicate my status
to every last syllable
otherwise, I'll never reach a 4.0
I study the perfections of her speech
no outstanding vowels in violation
unlike myself
and I vow to practice enunciation
and not trip over my words anymore
when the tip of my boot misses a lift in the
sidewalk
I've read that roots

will stretch in search of food
and lucky me,
I find the famished oak
we cross at the light
the shepherdess and her lambs
a flock in the pedestrian walk
I follow behind careful not to step
on her skirt as it flows
a mural of orange petals
bloom at her heels
she is a sprite
I am a frog
with a wish to ascend
the coveted baccalaureate tower
pray there aren't any bats
in the turret
a one hundred and thirty-two step climb
and on this staircase
mind the cobwebs
introduction to art
and it better be a brightly lit fortress
for surely,
I am not the next Picasso

make believe we're going on a picnic
she lowers herself
to the blades
and waves us to do the same
we settle down on the grass
in Silver Lake Park
but I haven't a basket
or a sandwich
or any fruit
and I doubt my mom or grandma

would approve
of sitting on the bare ground
without a blanket:
it's wet, you'll get a chill
and there's ants—they'll
crawl up your pants
and do a dance

it's still warm for late October
not at peak foliage
but the leaves have transformed
a few never made it to wardrobe
no chance to exchange for a crimson
or a golden
or technicolor coat
before the branches strip
as bare as the emperor
with a new set of clothes
I sketch
some new clothes before he
makes a spectacle of himself
parading in my notebook

it's best
the sprite instructs
as she glances my way
not to overthink the branches
remember, you're the branch
the tree
and the ground

maybe I'm the green grass too
to grow around
and around
I know about circles

I run a five-mile-long loop de loop
a tired Matchbox on a never-ending
track
quick, grab hold
why can't I stop spinning?

behold, the pencil
accompanies my fingers for a stroll
the branches stretch
and I no longer feel my arm
under me
the roots twist
till my feet are one
for now
I am planted
I am the arbor

WORM FODDER
I find a faded yellow receipt
as a bookmark
tucked between an ode
"To Some Buckets"
and "World War II"
or anything that surfaces
to separate pages can be a bookmark
to a bookworm
or at least an undergraduate
pretending to be one
and when I hold it
I'm a time walker
with my syllabus in hand
searching for my required books

by numbers
search by numbers never fails

once I connected the dots in a workbook
all the way to fifty and received a gold star
gold stars are best for fridges
I think as I pull
the book from the stand
new or used,
I choose new this time
because I want to be the first to navigate
its pages
just me and the virgin pages
waiting for the first touch
waiting for the magic to flow

I start to read while
I wait in line
about a man named Koch
talking to himself
about himself
and then answering himself
this is normal
I am normal
what is normal
about waiting in line
with stacks of books
we're told to read
and how to read
and discuss in a
designated amount of time
from a seat
in a row
in a room marked by a number

only accessed by the few
who've met the scholastic aptitude

regurgitation is used
by birds to feed their young
fill their empty little throats
with worms spit forth
I think I'm full
I'm probably full of regurgitated worms
I don't mind the belly
only the bloat

but there's a remedy—
a development of taste
I can sample whatever
I please
remark on the flavor
the texture
and the afterthought
since I have paid
for the books
continue to pay for the books
while I buy a book I like
when I like to
and sometimes I even
add my own name

~ for the love of *New Addresses*

A POET
a poet came to class
in brown trousers and
a tan sport coat without
any elbow patches

his button-down collar
unbuttoned

he unbuttons another button
exposing his undershirt and a bit
of chest hair
as the professor cracks a joke
not sure what kind of inside jokes
poets have
with other poets and if they speak
in meter
and is it iambic pentameter
or loose like a goose
on some chaotic chase?

the poet leans on the podium
it wiggles as he settles
his book against the lectern
I bought his book
it was listed in the syllabus and it's best to
get the recommended reading in
first
I flip the book over to discover that the professor
and the poet have matching labels
an exclusive club
of little houses
and I hope there isn't a gush of wind
or a tired old wolf with a rumbling in his belly
determined to blow them all down

when the poet reads
he bends each page behind the spine
reciting excerpts from
his life

in warm hues
some cold spots too
he pauses at the
end of each thought
not a rush to the finish line
I have thoughts like his
sometimes
these rambling thoughts
but my teachers taught
that run-on sentences were bad
never start with the word *but*
or *and*
try not to cross out
and if you must,
one line will do
and do not buy erasable pens
only a standard black or blue
forget red,
that's only for teachers
not students
the erasable pens are a waste
I am left with blue smudge on my hands
and how undelightful it is
to erase a mistake
I want to feel
the error of my ways
stand witness to a wreckage
of grammatical proportions

I flip through my notebook
and only find debris—
is there room
for me
any room for me

in the great libraries
with the great authors
and the great poets
even the small poets
with big voices
like the man who came to class
we all line up for an autograph

I want to be a writer, I address the man
in the earth-tone apparel
the man with the words
the published words
I regret my words immediately
the man without elbow patches
takes his book from my hand:
what is your name?

he hovers the pen
above the title page:
on the road to the self.
here's to the future!

there is no other answer
this is not specific enough
no footnotes
no citation
not even a critical analysis to follow
this is why I prefer the Oxford editions
I mark those up and add little adhesive flags
pink, green, yellow, blue
I go back and forth
to play tag

sixteen years later,
I find the book

and reread the autographed line
I think I have acquired a self,
poet man:
am I a writer now?

PROFESSOR WHO?

dear professor,
please excuse me as I
romanticize
about your suede
elbow patches

dear god of the syllabus,
the maker or breaker of my GPA
I follow your lips
when you read aloud
and I know
that you know
you are the superb
being of prose
an expert of those by Foster
and Brown
and how to place
in-text citations
you emphasize the need
to double-space
add a half-inch indentation
for subsequent lines
on the works-cited list

dear man behind the podium,
when you prop your foot up
on the stool

to lean into my question
do you mind
if I ask
why the need to be taller
when you speak to me

dear father of the pass/fail option,
what about the time I dropped
my quarters and dimes and a few pennies
at the counter
while I ordered my English Breakfast tea
and you your coffee, black
in the little café
where you often read the *Times*
that afternoon you bent down to pick
up my stray quarters
and smiled at me
when our eyes met
and our fingers
touched at the tips
thank you, I said

as you walked away
olive duster swept closed
you paused
to flatten your lapel
and reaffirm
my pupils
held the display
of you, professor,
in their frame

Adventures with a Man
Seven Years Older

....

THE TEST

Winter 2001: An Education

"What's this?"

He picks up my textbook, *Educational Foundations*. The man I've been dating—our acquaintance began in a chat room, progressed with AIM, and graduated to my grandparents' basement—happens to be a few years my senior. He's Gen X, so I'll forgive him for thinking *90210* is better than *Dawson's Creek*.

"It's about the founders in education. The forerunners, the forefathers. Theories and practical applications."

He flips the pages with his thumb. Like the guys in the movies, who sit at folding tables counting wads of cash while smoke fills the air and there's usually a large clock on the wall.

"I've flagged them by theory. This tab is for social constructivists. See here, this is Piaget." I point to a pink Post-it.

"And this one, well, I like him above the rest. This one is Vygotsky." The theorist of the zone of proximal development deserves a green Post-it.

"You like to study?" He takes the book from my hand and places me on his lap. The textbook lands cover-up on the floor. There's a picture of students sitting in rows and an eager teacher ready to call on one of the many hands that are raised before her. My partner has been doing his own studying. All over me.

I pick up my book and adjust my sweater.

"I like to pass, mostly. I want to pass on the first try."

"What is it with you and having a first? Want to hold on to your newness forever?"

Somehow, I don't think he's talking about my test.

"I have to pass so I can get to the next test. And then I will be closer to my certification. I can teach anywhere in New York City, it's the ticket in."

"You really think you're going to pass?" He strokes his chin, cocking his head to the side.

I envision one of those anvils, the kind used in Saturday morning cartoons. It's shiny and it leaves a crater in the floor when it's dropped.

"Yes, I studied and studied till my eyes hurt."

"You're not going to pass," he says as a matter of fact, reaching for his coat.

I didn't realize it's possible for steam to rise from my head.

"Want to bet?"

Spoiler alert: I passed.

THE PROPOSAL

Spring 2002: The Phone Call

Man: I like you, but you're too young for me.

Me: It didn't seem to bother you when we first met.

Man: But I need sex.

Me: As you remind me each time we're together.

Man: You can't expect me— I have to go out with other girls.

Me: Thanks for your consideration.

Man: But you're marriage material.

Me: What the fuck does that mean?

Man: You're going to be a good wife and mother.

Me: How do you know?

Man: I can just tell.

Me: I'm EIGHTEEN, and I'm not marrying anybody right now.

Man: Yeah, but in a couple of years—

Me: Years?

Man: We'll stay friends.

Me: So, let me get this correct. I'm going to wait here until YOU'RE
   ready to get married?

Man: Sure, why not?

Me: Should I get my knitting needle?

Man (laughing): So, I'll give you a call sometime?

Me: I'm good. Bye.

CENTER STAGE

I hate Bs

I only want As

but why is an A better than a B?

is it because she comes at the

front of the line?

is there something wrong
with being second?

I like second course
it fills me more
than the appetizer ever can
so why do I crave
the ecstasy of an A
when I'm destined
to chase her
my entire existence
never able to return
to the front of the line
landing further down the
row of letter importance
somewhere around the letters
w or is it q
embarrassed to count back
and review
because I hike miles of
rigid lines on a mountain
too steep to climb
slide down with every try
and forget the beauty of a curve
the thrill of a dip
the tail of a g
hold on
and swing
grab for the vines
be the Tarzan
of my own design

———

but who am I kidding?
I hate the idea
of a drop
hate to fall
rather prick a finger
on the pointed tip
of an A
spill the blood
watch it run down
the sides
congratulations will follow
from the blood I've drawn
and now I may frame it
because I am the best
I deserve to be mounted
in the center of the wall

AGAIN, AGAIN
hit me again,
I whisper to the computer screen as
I log in my student ID
and I'm completely original
using my birthday as the passcode
ready to be released from this prison
of *do I* or *don't I*
have another semester on the dean's list
I put last semester's congratulatory letter signed
by the dean on the fridge under
grandma's special magnet—
a lady with a red hat and a purple feather
in her hair made my letter look better than

a million bucks
if I had that kind of cash
I'd forget all about my GPA
and take a vacation to Rome
and throw my newfound wealth into the
Trevi Fountain
but that's absurd
I close my eyes
make a wish
and move the arrow to the box marked
SPRING 2004

(scroll down)

A
ah!
A
more!
A
again, again!
A
don't stop, I'm almost there!
A
oh God!
A
!!!!!

WALL ART
come and see my wall art
I have my own museum
I bet you didn't think
a girl in a two-story
side-hall colonial

no marble floors
or guardian lion statues
could own
a museum somewhere
in the wilds of suburbia
(don't ask about the taxes)
but she does,
I do

here, look upon my wall
and don't speak too loudly
or she'll awake from her slumber
her gold seal affixed, she shines
behind the glass
in her bed of matted finish
the headboard
the footboard
the side rails
all mahogany

with her, I may go off and conquer
the world
for I have my shield
my bachelor's degree
more specifically, my B.S. Ed.
to polish
and my fortress
to climb
the top of the endless
pile
for awhile
until the shine wears
like the glow of an evening gown
after a few cocktails

and the mascara leaves a trail
of black smudge
as a souvenir

she got lonely
she did
and what kind of a person would I be
if I didn't please her
and seek out a companion
to balance the wall

and so, visitor
don't worry,
we have time for this tale,
no need for a closing hour
I spun around
again,
the academic clock
tick, tock
tick, tock
don't stop to knock

here's another,
see her there?
the companion, she sleeps too,
a bit taller, she prefers the crown
and demands her title heard
above the crowd
MS, she declares
(don't forget the ED)
her crown is crooked but I
won't be the one to inform her
she who holds the staff
it's gold

her kingdom comes at an expense:
six digits and
multiple zeros

but would you believe it?
I couldn't
the complaints that followed:
it's not enough
they cried
two why two?
we want more company

I didn't argue
no, no
they were right
I should be fair
what's another bundle to love?
a syllabus to cradle in my arms
check off each assignment
post to the board
a daily post to the board
and what's with all the virtual insanity?
I want chalk
I want to make beautiful cursive
all over that green
or black or blue board
it doesn't matter the size

and then came the third member
there she is
next to her sisters
and their frames
isn't she lovely?
and more reason too

for the extra zeros tacked on
will wear as long
as I breathe air

you'd think the trio is satisfied with
a pair of twins?
but oh, no
no, no
double trouble
they fight over who's got
the better M and the better S
and yes, you can guess,
even the E and the D
the first, well, she gave up entirely
she says,
I'm better off letting them
duke it out
she doesn't want to
chip her frame
vain she is,
vain as a rose

no time to fret
I think, somehow,
I think I came up
with an excellent solution
another one should balance it out,
don't you agree
that even is better than odd
any day of the week,
am I right?
come back,
I'll pour you
some tea

herbal is helpful, no?
(hand on doorknob)

wait,
before you leave,
(hasty little thing)
let me show you
how I dust my frames
and did I ever tell you about the time
there was a little spider
that climbed inside
and frightened me
when I inspected the
summa cum laude inscription?

I never noticed
he became a permanent
fixture

SEVEN

BE THEIR GUEST

FRAMES
she kept him
in a frame
my great-great aunt in the nursing home

that's my D—
there he is—a handsome man, don't you think?

she taps the gold-trimmed frame on
the nightstand
by her bed
it's a simple bed
barely a full size
more of a twin
not that she
needs much space
she's as thin as the rail
that protects her from falling at
night while she dreams
in clouds of

white
white sheets
white pillows
white pillowcases
and an afghan on top streaming with red and
yellow thread

I'd say so,
he looks sharp in his uniform

hat tilted to the side
an inch above his brow
three stripes along the collar
and he wore a
moustache like a lamp shade
neatly trimmed
but mostly he wore the
cleft on his chin
she had a string of pearls
and her hair pinned back
in soft curls

a navy man, he was
and a good one too
oh, he was a good man
my D—

you must miss him

every day, she says,
every day since he left me

what's it like to be alone
in a bed
in a room
that's not your own

with only pictures to take
do the pictures come and go
like a slideshow
in your head?

was he your best friend?

the best
once I was out with my girlfriends
we walked on the beach
and there were men who came
and joined us
we took off our shoes to go in the water
but I only stood up to my ankles
because it was that time of the month
and I told them, no, I don't want to go in
and they tried to throw me in
clothes and all
but it was D— who got them to stop

lucky then?

lucky? I married him
that's us on our wedding day

she points to a photo above her
white bed
her finger is bent a little at the
tip and I wonder how long she's been pointing
at him
her bouquet of calla lilies joins them at the hip
there's blush at her cheeks
plump lips with a tint of pink
the groom's hair parted to the side
a dollop of pomade tames his wavy locks

———

I'm going to see him soon
she stares at the wall past the frame
her smile is gone and
I'm not going to argue with her
I'm not a timekeeper,
I hate watches anyhow

the next morning, the phone rings,
I pick up

it's Aunt—
I announce to my mom and grandma
while they sit at the kitchen table
having a cup of morning coffee

I want to die
I want to go home
she tells me
over and over
and the words repeat
like the calliope music of
a carousel
home
home
die
die

the phone calls repeat
the day after
the day after that
for a week
we visit her
we call
we ask the staff to stop her

from calling
but she needs him
she needs to find her D—
and she doesn't stop

the answering machine is full
when I get home from class
I'm told to erase it, it's Aunt—
but to erase I must listen first:
I want to die
I want to go home

she repeats over and over
home
home
die
die
her plea received
by the great phone above
and she went home
I hope
she found her love

a box of photos came back
to us
she had no next of kin
and the photos sat there
he, in his uniform
she, in her pearls
the both of them with a bouquet
of calla lilies
I adopt them so they stay
alive in stories
they stay alive by name

———

I will
bequeath them to my daughter and then she will
bequeath them to her daughters
and they can keep them safe and me too
and now I will
go to the craft store and search through shelves
of frames and choose one
that compliments my skin tone

SUBURBAN SHADE
I'm an expert at living
in squares
of appropriated land
funded by the tears
of the nine-to-fivers
Gen-X and Y-ers
bought by a long-distance
commute

where April deadlines loom
and squiggle lines are drawn
across foreheads
and creases carve
into corners of weary eyes
plummet into dark pools
and lengthen their stay
on the deep end

when the bloom
of hopes and dreams
among the dazed and confused
days of youth

fade with the onset
of the dreaded middle age
I sit
and wait

this safety net I weaved
has wrapped itself around my neck
and I can no longer breathe
an existence of perimeters
among white post soldiers
pulling rank
whether weathered or brand-new
they're sent to divide me
from my friendship with the sun
and the air is stale
from disillusioned brides and grooms
fighting in the bedroom
their voices carry in the wind
and land in my backyard
along with the regrets of toddlers
waving bye, bye mommy
and hello daddy,
the weekend warrior

my stationary army
grows higher each day
and I shrink
when I taste my chemically dependent
but aesthetically appealing
patches of green space
sprawling to the rooted feet
of the giants
standing thick-bellied in pride
laughing as their insides burst

with robins' nests, spiders,
and the buzzing of bees
all on parade
in front of the white-post brigade

the magic only lasts
for a moment or two
until I find the weeds
that stick out along the perimeter
they stand up and point out
my lack of thumbs

while I wait
legs folded
ready to sprout seeds
to match the rows
these garden lanes
protected by suburban shade

ALL THE WHILE
sometimes the words flow
from a faucet
and I enjoy the waterfall
as it mingles with my hair
in the shower
and I can pretend I'm
a rock star
getting ready for the press
my latest release is coming out
and I'm on top
nothing will stop me

———

sometimes the drain is clogged
and I yank out hair clumps
until my head hurts
and my brain is scrambled
up good and fluffy
not over easy
and the only thing I can do
is surf
swim the stream of so-called reality
life at the Jersey Shore
tans and tropical island oil that smells like
coconuts and sex
lots of sex
and reruns
lots of reruns especially the covered wagon
kind with Ma and Pa and Mary and
Laura
and the best season is when
she falls in love with Almanzo
and
I
want
nothing
to
do
with a notebook or a pen
or a book
or read anything at all
unless it involves the *Post*
page 6, celebrity news

———

and I'll transform
into a social media harlot
pinning recipes
linen tablecloths
and the fireman from
the latest calendar
too hot to handle
on my fridge

when I'd finally had my fill
of the dumpster dive
I hunger for her
and I hunt
belly down on the ground
dressed in camouflage
with my tripod and camera
wait for the elusive creature to arrive
and it's a scene out of *Wild America*,
Marty Stouffer–style
except for the beard
although I do appreciate a man with a beard
there's this primal urge to procreate
and my ovaries are bursting
egg whites
the healthy kind
that makes babies with great
curls
that land in the middle of the forehead
and I am joyful to hold the bouncing
little bundle of joy in my lap
until the joy overflows onto my shirt
and adds more bags under my eyes

and less time for the page
which I will chase
endlessly for
more space
on my kitchen table
to rest my elbows
and create
perfect juxtaposition
syntax
or is it semantics
and use onomatopoeia
and other literary terms that my AP English teacher
taught me in high school
all the while being underpaid
so that one day
or once upon a big fat
fictional fantasyland maybe
I'll achieve
selling power
get rich
pay my taxes on time
and read a lifetime
of really good books
off a list assigned
for incoming freshman
those by Charlotte or Jane
who I will never sound like
not even with the aid of Merriam-Webster
but wish I could
hear voices calling in the wind or dance
with a man too proud

———

and then I'll read those notoriously bad books
that no one wants to admit
they blushed over a man with a secret room
and way too much money to spend
on a plain girl who
fades into the scenery like drapes,
this shower curtain keeps me safe

and all of this I must do
before I die
but first wonder to myself

where is my shampoo?

SOMEWHERE IN THE BERKSHIRES
PART I: DEAR HENRY

he had the best room,
the docent remarks
our group stops to stare
a crowd in the hallway,
phones in the upright position
capturing images of preserved
importance while we rattle off
a list of questions:
did he visit often?
where did he sit?
what kind of ink did he use?
did he keep company late at night?

the docent answers and nods
politely
as polite as can be

when the questions
all the questions
float around
like a bunch of
busy bees

I suppose she doesn't know it all
no ghouls of literati
roaming the halls
moaning their tales
wailing at the guests
flicking the switches
and sliding down the banister
I don't know why they'd want to slide
down the banister but
I like to imagine Edith and Henry
dressed up for dinner
waiting for an unsuspecting guest
preferably a nosy one
with too many questions
and they come sliding down
screaming *boooo* and
oooo and other cliché ghost noises
and just like that, bam,
no more questions

they can scare me
as much as they please
I'll be a snoop, anyhow
I try on my best version
of a second-rate
Nancy Drew from Jersey
forget that,
I'm not much

of a sleuth
if I had a real detective eye
I'd discover the secret
to Henry's room
the secret of the Mount
for those invited to
Edith's place
brought thoughts to paper
paper to novel
novel to press at a private desk
there were notes from Wharton to her guest
and an empty chair
the chair had a sign:
DO NOT SIT
of course, you may not sit,
silly creature,
you have no invitation
peasant girl,
you
are
not
a
guest

come along,
the docent announces,
to her group of
enthusiastic tourists with
equally enthusiastic phones
the group proceeds in a line
one woman likes to keep behind
the docent and adjust the lens
on her camera

she nudges me with her elbow
in the doorway
outside of Henry's room
pardon me, world renown photographer
for being in the frame
I have never sort fame
but I stay by his door to inquire
a bit more

dear Henry,
what would you say,
if I asked to stay?
do you think she would mind if a girl,
a girl like me,
bunked overnight?
a sleepover would
be fun, I'll bring popcorn, we can play
charades and
I'm as quiet as a mouse,
I assure,
you won't hear a peep
unless you want to chat
have a nightcap
and we can exchange
ghost stories by the fireplace
scare me, go ahead,
I've been to Bly
more than once
and survived
faces lurking through
dining room windows

dear Henry,
tell me your secret,

of how to dine with the Joneses,
sit elbow-to-elbow with Mary
and Beatrix
discuss matters of the grounds,
Mr. Berry at your side
there must be much to say
about perennials

the group is almost out of sight
I'm getting a wave
and I'm afraid I'll get lost on this tour
of literary greatness

dear Henry,
I need to find a way to write
in bed just like Edith
she told you that, right?
if I stay
I can number the pages
as my thoughts spill out
and they will spill better
when you and Edith are near
and when I use a glass jar
with ink and a nib to dip
pardon my drippings on
the embroidered quilt
and onto the floor they will sail
my very own snail mail
I will employ a staff member
to pick them up
perhaps the ginger tabby
that lounges in the sunbeams
at my back door,
he will collect them

number by number
neatly stacked and
ready and waiting
that will work
it has to work

do you agree, Henry?
and if I stay, I'll never have to worry
about what to eat
because that's what the dumbwaiter is for
have the butler bring it to me
no hands of mine will touch a stove
I suppose it would be nice
not to worry about cleaning
the splotches of yolk
that run from the skillet
while I record my thoughts
in the Notes application
of my phone and
catch those slippery thoughts
throw a lasso
before they slip away

then I may spend the rest of the day
in my library of first editions
while away my afternoon as a scholiast
margins are delicious spaces for thoughts
I won't bother with those pesky sticky notes
no, just pencil away at the sides
for dessert, Austen will do
she has a few copies in here
bet they have notes too

———

dear Henry,
time is running out
on this autumn afternoon
and I wonder
if we can take a turn about the gardens
we can stroll alongside the trees
meander down the lane
I like that word, *meander,*
it's thesaurus-friendly
and marvel
at the lime
and I may remark
about the fountain
by the rectangular pond
and you will discuss her fondness for dahlias
and delphiniums
but Henry, I must interrupt,
the clock has expired
the doors will close
and still
no invitation to hold

dear Henry,
I must ask a final favor
can you put in
a good word for me?
we've gotten to know
each other today
and only you understand
I have but one request
just ask her, Henry, be bold
just ask, dear Edith,

if she would be so kind
to make a place for me
for the former New York girl
she knows the kind
remind her about the Brant girl,
the one of her design

PART II: BE THEIR GUEST

at first it was only me
and the Steinway
the Steinway is famous
because it comes with an autograph
not all pianos are boastful
but this one is a peacock
with gold plumes
making a spectacle of itself
in the parlor
that's the old-timey term
for where the folks of the house
used to let their guests mingle about and
smoke and talk and in this particular setting,
fawn all over the
Steinway with a Hollywood résumé

and to assure
that the guests of the bed-and-breakfast
are properly convinced
of the authenticity of the pretty scribble,
the date and time are also inscribed
there's even a small bio
about the composer
whose nimble fingers
danced upon the Bavarian spruce keys

and of course, I looked that up,
what the hell would I know
about a Steinway?
I had a Casio keyboard
as a kid
and I only played the demo function
but as a guest, oh,
what a treat
I am a witness to the very spot
where the pretty scribble man
wowed a group of guests
with his ensemble
about a girl who rose
from the sea
and a man-turned-beast who
kept a rose with temperamental
petals under glass

the afternoon is promising
I prepare to spend it
alongside the Steinway and its
homage to pretty scribbles
and decided to make some scribbles of my own
in my notebook
not pretty of course,
no accompanying authentication
more like the doodles of girl
with a fetish for the poet
she is honoring this week
pish posh,
doesn't matter, not to the Steinway
and me
we're like buddies

fast growing friends delighting
in one another's company
I sit,
she gathers dust,
no one complains

if only that was the case,
but the Steinway and I,
we became three
in walked,
more like waltzed,
Mrs. Cardigan Sweater or
whatever and a pair of brown trousers
if only my mother could see these trousers,
these are the kind of pants that make
fashion designers dig a hole to
bury their heads
she's a preferred guest,
I presume
she didn't even say hello
to the Steinway
not even an acknowledgment
of a glance, rude,
rude cardigan
super rude
trousers

I thought,
maybe,
that was the end
of the rude garments
but no
ruder yet,

the shoes
she removes her flats
and flings them one,
thud
after another,
thud
and then the socks
Mrs. Cardigan swings her feet
over the arm of a faded blue
love seat I remember the time
I put my feet over the arm
of my grandma's couch
and my mother
and my grandma sang·
DO NOT
the stuffing will get unstuffed
the spring will get sprung
the couch will sink
and then
it
will
be
done

but Mrs. Cardigan does not appear to
have had a grandma or a mom to warn
her of the tragic consequences
to upholstery
she wiggles her toes
they have red polish
she admires the red polish
her legs sprawled out

on the love seat
a show pillow
wedged behind her head

Mrs. Cardigan holds up
a glass
can you guess?
red plucked from the best of vines
and she says:
it's a good day for wine

yes, I reply
I indulge her because
this is the accepted response
for bed-and-breakfast social protocol
that I agree with a total stranger in a cardigan
make niceties with a total stranger in brown trousers
while her red-polished toes
are free to roam

it isn't fair,
I tell the Steinway,
I want leisure toes and free soles
no matter a callous
or unpolished nature
let them roam wild
explore mountains and valleys and hills
but not all hills
not that one hill in town
the one Ethan went down
a last thrill ride
although it didn't go quite as planned
thanks to a tree
but that's what you'll get

for fancy free
feet
or too much
wine
or too much
time
I better stick
to my doodles

Mrs. Cardigan has returned
to an upright position
her glass is empty
she returns her toes
to her socks
and her socks to her shoes

there is pâté in the dining room
an announcement is made
to Mrs. Cardigan from
Mrs. Turtleneck
and another
pair of trousers
as for me,
I am yet to receive an invitation

THE BENT KNEE OBSERVER
I love when you tell me
no
I love when you say
there's
no
way
keep to your corner,

little spider
or they'll crush you
under the weight
of their boots
salt sticks in the grooves
left over from last year
and years before
storms rage
a war in your brain
blue sticks
to your collar
try to remove it
they'll see
right through it

lurch
urchin, lurch
find the steerage deck
there'd be
no helm for you
keep to the crow's nest
how about
a good sweep of the street
little you
it's a thick sea of creatures
crystal blue and deep green
and you're a lonely
black dot

back to spinning
your web,
watch
those pretty knees

———

maybe
I'm a silly little
bent knee observer
maybe
I'm a tragic tale
maybe
I'm lost
on a trail of beginnings
an endless loop of
maybe
I'm a wasteland
of dust bunnies
waiting around for the
mercy
of a vacuum nozzle
destined to roll
around the living room
floor
hide under couches
behind curtains
watch the hands
change hour
while I count down
to the next rotation

EIGHT

The Caffeinated End

TIPSY DOODLE

Tipsy Doodle
she lost her noodles
oodles and oodles
onto the floor

she picks them up
they fall back down
with a flip, flop
her socks are wet
she soaks all day
and drips all night

don't look,
look away
and don't come back
till she's right to play . . .

GLIDER TALE

I sit on the glider
she lies on my chest
as these days
they fly
one into the next
no magic sand
no fairy dust
no thimble to kiss
no wish to grant
a goodnight lullaby
she cries
I follow the walls
they lie
baby lifts her chin
and somehow
she knows
mommy, mommy
why are you
such a mess?

I study my firstborn
but I'm afraid
she'll be swept away
by the sad surging
in Atlantic strength
waves tear into the nursery
only this glider
can keep the both of us afloat
our own little safety boat
oh, mother dear
pull yourself together

come on, woman
you're not the first
and you most certainly
won't be the last

but the walls
are judging me
a pudgy bear
with an incurable taste
for honey
and his buddy,
a timid and little pig
an unusual alliance
shake their heads
what an unfeeling woman!
let's throw her
far from the enchanted forest!
she doesn't belong here,
she doesn't deserve her!
banish her! banish her!
leave her to wither away
to a rotten pulp!

excuse me, wall marauders,
raiders of the nursery
can you keep a secret, innocent creatures
that creep alongside my baby's room
whom of my own accord, my own hands
flattened to the pale yellow
and neutral green wall?
I feel that you may be right, after all.
what is to be done, dear judgmental figments?
what will I become?
a monster

an ogre
something hairy with multiple legs, claws,
and fangs?

pink and timid tugs
at the red shirt of the pudgy bear
that scratches his exposed
and round belly:
she is lost,
she is found
she is bound to be
where the well
ends round

dear, dearest
forest dwellers
who's lost?
I'm here, aren't I?
and you are only
the remnants of progesterone
as she vacates
you will be left
longing to tug
at my ear
go bother with your honey
bother with your wall
you may leave me

at three a.m.
aboard a glider
sits baby and me
our lullaby at sea

ELASTIC BAND

I am an elastic band
you like to wear
stretch me by hand
wait for the tear

come and pluck my rubber bits
from the carpeting
worn to bare soles without slippers
and snug toes
pop out from the sock
riddled with holes
begin to sprout
shoots to grow into
trees with limbs too weak to keep
from falling
asleep

collect me piece by piece
lay me in a circle
to run around
and around
wait for the sound
of the cuckoo
chimes but no
clock to be found
but
duck
duck
take cover

the goose has vacated the building

THE BROOM, THE CLOSET,
AND A STACK OF LAUNDRY

lazy!
the broom screams at me
from the corner of the room

you're a beast—a hairy
beastly beast!
stop pointing out my dust bunnies
they want to be bunnies
let them be bunnies
to hop
kick out their furry little feet
and skip along a spider's lair
leap up the staircase
climb towards the moonlight
second star to the right
that I can only dream to reach
but not really
because who wants to fly to dust
no way
I only fly
when I have fairy dust
and fairy dust should never be wasted
on cobwebs

I believe,
do you hear?
I point
at the broom
that you, beastly, have no
power over me

———

oh, yeah?
says the closet.
try again
I can make you twitch
I bet I
can make you squirm

you may try
but I will go through
my wardrobe
and find:
half a goat, half a man
and he'll lead me to a snowy land

cough, cough
the malicious ogre spills a decade
of shoes all over the hardwood
floor (why do I still
own jellies and clogs?)

try me once more
and I will never
dust your shelves again
yes, shelves in the closet
will make me laugh
and think of
Lizzie Bennet and
how she escaped a fate worse
than a summer's day spent fawning
over you

but I have you forever!
a laugh resounds
from down the hall

the worst
of them all
a bloodsucker more
fearsome than
a dark-haired, stalk-the-night
sharp-toothed villain
out of an Anne Rice
novel
it's the laundry pile

you're mine, day after day
why deny it?
why fight it?
dive in
and let me love you
bath towels stacked
high
underwear with princesses
dressed in pastels
and dreams of wealthy
castle owning
men
and a whole bunch of
dishcloths

I will climb the kitchen counter
and lie across you
spill my words
on top of you
and I won't tell a soul
of how you lost
your threads
to the feisty machine

in the laundry room
and how she tossed you like
a buoy in the eye
of a storm
but you secretly loved
every minute?

ha! why bother with words?
I'll keep you company
boasts the dryer with a mouthful
of boxer shorts
two t-shirts
all kinds of
socks (I hate it when they go missing and I have to check
the lint screen)
and my lacy bra

because
she will always find a way,
silence her
and she will burst from the walls
and scare you as
she slinks across your floors
be gone, broom
be gone, closet
be gone, washer
and dryer
and a pile of dishcloths
leave me
to my dust

THE CAFFEINATED END

three o'clock
and not a drop remains
in either leg
I dangle my feet
over a daffodil-yellow
fireside chair
an arm
across my face
with a distaste
for the sun
in its peppy step

it's the afternoon
when I find myself
alone
in a teacup
trapped within its brown tide
while I wait
the fog recedes
and frightens the cobwebs away

and that's when I
catch me
about my own fare
devilish fare
ask me what I think
but I don't care
not a spoonful
not a worry
not even a lump
of sugar's worth

———

I jump in
when a short-tempered wave
knocks me
and I fall to my knees
and disappear
yes, vanish
onto the leveled countertop

ah, it's fifteen past three
and the more I drink
the stronger the desire
the blackest of brews

ask me, who
ask me, why
I cannot hear over the sound
of my sipping
and please, do sip it
don't gulp it, dear

it's rather easy
when the warmth encourages
my lips to the brim
I can fit right in
and how it's good
how satisfyingly good
to find myself
floating

I'd never wish to stop
but then
no longer a drop
I rejoice at my own
disposal—

I don't mind
greeting myself
at the caffeinated
end

such a happy girl
in a perfect world
I agree for the moment:

isn't it a lovely day?

NINE

FAIRY WINGS

I AM THE WIND
the wind unzips the screen from its track
along the canopy that shields
my three-year-old and me
from hungry winged creatures
that stalk the backyard

we sit on chairs
with white anchors sewn
into navy cushions
and use markers
to color magic inside
a unicorn prancing
in a fairy garden
while we resist the touch
of ultraviolet rays
the wind invites itself to stay
for company

and it is my daughter
who brings
the welcoming committee

I hug the wind
she declares
her arms open
to embrace the warmth
of an August breeze
as it blankets her
she places her arms across
her chest covering the sunbeam
design on her tangerine shirt
she doesn't mind when the wind
tousles her hair
blue eyes sparkle
beneath the wisps of
chestnut locks

I kiss the wind
she blows a kiss
into the palm of her hand
releases love
into the wilderness
where it may choose
to float above the fence posts
the chimney stack
or hitch a ride on
a nearby cloud

when the wind
is calling
listen

open the windows
open the doors
and direction will flow
like the sea
to the stars

The Clinic

It is quiet in the living room. Maybe a little too quiet. When the source of quiet is a four-year-old, the quiet becomes a questionable quiet, the kind of quiet that often spells t-r-o-u-b-l-e. Thirty-eight inches of quiet is standing beside the couch. She wears a unicorn headband with a silver horn and an attached crown of pink flowers. There is a purple stethoscope at her neckline with a pink chest-piece. The ear tips are in place, and she is ready for work. The patient waits on the cushion. He watches closely as she approaches, his golden eyes widen, and the tip of a striped tail twitches. The unicorn-clad physician places the round pink bell on her furry patient and gives me a raise of her eyebrow. One eyebrow is all it takes.

"Mommy," she says, holding up her hand, "you can't be here."

"I'm sorry, do I need an appointment?" I sit next to the patient. He stretches a paw onto my lap.

"Yes," she says, her horn leaning forward. "I'm the doctor. The animal doctor."

"So that's a no for your mother?"

"Sorry, Mommy. Only Oliver."

"Oh, I see. What ails the patient?"

"What does that mean?" The doctor scrunches her nose.

"It means what makes you feel sick."

"This is a check-up, Mommy."

The doctor waves her hand for me to move off the couch.

"Ba-bump. Ba-bump. Ba-bump." She places emphasis on the *ba* before the *bump*. The stethoscope is resting on the white fur of the patient's belly. The tabby raises his head to look at me, his whiskers have grown longer, like the sides of a handlebar moustache.

"It's time for a shot."

It's fortunate that most cats do not speak fluent human. Aside from the few terms for food—say "turkey," and he'll come running, say "tuna fish," and he'll downright lose his feline mind—and a few of my rules—"no, get off the counter, no, don't scratch my couch" (he ignores me)—Oliver lives in a world of afternoon siestas. But if he suspects his soon-to-be fate, I'm sure there'll be a dash to the highest cabinet in the kitchen.

"I'll be right back." She walks across the room and opens the lid of a trunk decorated in bright pink and yellow flowers. In seconds, a wardrobe collects on the hardwood floor. A pair of yellow and orange fairy wings, a blue dress with a white apron, a gold dress with pink roses embroidered on the waist, and a silver crown.

The doctor returns, clacking the floor of her office. Her heels have a design of a mouse wearing a pink bow with white polka dots. For a final touch, completing her physician's ensemble, a silky fuchsia and purple skirt rests over her peach leggings.

Clutching a sparkly purple and white doctor bag, she reaches in and pulls out a plastic syringe. With the plunger pulled back in firing position, she aims the rounded, pink needle tip in the direction of her furry patient. On cue, Oliver jumps off the couch. I presume this may not be his first check-up.

"Look, Mommy." She twirls around, stethoscope in flight. "I'm dancing and I'm a doctor." She pauses for a moment and creases her eyebrows. "Do doctors dance?"

"They can dance if they want to."

"Can doctors wear high heels? And do ba-bump, ba-bump?" She places the stethoscope on my chest.

"Doctors can wear whatever they like except when they perform surgery."

She crinkles her nose. "What's surge-knee?"

"Surgery? That's when a doctor takes a patient to the hospital to help fix a boo-boo. The doctor will wear special clothes called scrubs to make sure that everyone stays clean and germ-free."

"Oh." She looks down at her feet. One heel on, the other heel abandoned near the sparkly on-the-go doctor kit.

"Mommy?"

"Yes?"

"I think maybe I want to be a doctor too. When I'm older." She places a hand on her hip.

"I think if you want to be a doctor, you can be a doctor."

She smiles at me, placing the tip of the plastic syringe in the rear of a stuffed dog wearing an orange baseball cap.

It appears that all is resolved. Career choice probable, and a tabby cat well taken care of—his heart is ba-bumping, and life is as it should be. But there's that quiet again. The quiet stretches from underneath the couch. Next to a lonely miniature teacup, one without its matching saucer—oh, that's where it went—there lies a curled fluff of tan fur with stripes. A pair of gold eyes greets my own. He regrets to inform that he does not agree with the current consensus.

FREEZE

there are four swings
in the playground

she holds up her hand
and hides her thumb

—

I try to pump
but I'm too slow
teacher says practice
and then my friend and I
play tic–tac–toe

she spins in a circle
to weave her tale

wild boys, mommy,
there are wild lion boys
who chase us girls
around

I wipe a smear of chocolate
from her cheek a
leftover cookie trail
she pats my hand away

and around the green slide
where they roar but I
climb the stairs and
wiggle like a snake
until I touch the ground

she sits on the floor
her chin resting
on her knees

you must be tired

no, there's more
there's a seesaw
its seat is red
I sit in the middle because I

can't push high
like the other girls
and I can't hang
from the monkey bars
with one hand
I let go
and be a unicorn

a unicorn?

for magic dust and rainbow power
and then I play superhero
and run fast

she takes a lap
around the couch

and faster and hide behind
the tree

she hides
behind the bookcase

is the tree tall?

the leaves fall from the top
green
brown
yellow
orange

her fingers dance
an autumn jig
tapping our living room floor

and mommy
I am brave

when the lions roar
and when the
class has to freeze

she stops
puts her hands to her side
like wooden soldiers
on parade

freeze dance?

no

freeze tag?

teacher says
FREEZE for cars

cars?

cars that come up
the road

the road?

the little road
to see the stones

what stones?

the Jesus stones
teacher says
never touch the Jesus stones
and don't
go on the grass

the stones are special?

the stones have letters

the stones have numbers
and a rose

a rose?

a lady planted a flower by the Jesus
stone

she kneels on the rug by
our back door and presses
her hands
on the floral pattern

why?

it's for the people who died
and gone to heaven
like daddy's grandma
and your grandma
and remember the time you cried?

I do

because you miss her?

I do

because you can't see her anymore?

I nod because if I say another word
I fear
I will unleash a waterfall
and wash away
the roses

mommy?

yes?

———

we'll go to her Jesus stone

the kindergartner
places her hand
on mine

THE LAST THOUGHT ON THE TURTLE
turtle, oh, turtle dear
I thought about you
the other day
when my family and I
drove over
the Outerbridge Crossing

you're gone by now
off to turtle heaven but not before
you made turtles of your own
and they're out in the marsh
making mud pies with great herons
wading, one leg bent,
to grab a fish dinner

my daughter wanted to know
what made me smile
from ear to ear when we drove
past Mulberry Avenue
I told her about you
and the pink Band-Aid
she laughed

mommy, turtles don't wear Band-Aids

About the Author

Jaclyn Cohen is a bookworm extraordinaire and a Bookstagram fanatic. When she's not reading, Jaclyn is writing about fickle protagonists who enjoy lighting her outlines on fire. She manages to contain her composure through a daily regimen of peppermint tea, poetry, yoga (followed by chocolate chip cookies), and running her own dog bed-and-breakfast, Furtastic Friends and Boarding. This is an added bonus, as her furry houseguests act as co-editors. The tabby cat on the premises has refused to make any comments.

A native Staten Islander who paid her fair share of tolls, Jaclyn moved over the bridge and settled in Monmouth County, New Jersey. She encourages her daughter's bookworm behavior with weekly mommy-daughter book club meetings and the goal of turning their home into a personal library. The husband prefers not to comment on the household's book-buying budget.

Don't Go Over The Bridge is Jaclyn's first full-length poetry and short story collection. She is currently writing her first novel.

Made in United States
Orlando, FL
07 May 2023

32891936R00129